THE TRAVELLER'S INTERNET GUIDE

Travel the world
on the web

Contributors

Jonathan Lorie is the Editor of *Traveller* magazine and *The Traveller's Handbook*. **Amy Sohanpaul** is a staff writer and food columnist on *Traveller* magazine and Assistant Editor of *The Traveller's Handbook*. **Chris Martin** is Managing Editor of The Bookplace, an online bookstore, and its online magazines.

Online updates

An online version of this book, including updates, can be found at www.wexas.com/internetguide (for WEXAS members) or at www.travelleronline.com/internetguide (for non-members). Please email any corrections or updates to us at publicationseditor@wexas.com.

Also available

The Traveller's Handbook: the insider's guide to world travel offers expert advice and a comprehensive factual directory on how to travel anywhere, anyhow. £14.99

The Traveller's Healthbook: the pocket guide to worldwide health is an easy-to-use guide on every aspect of travel health, from tummy troubles to tropical diseases, from sunburn to snake bites. £7.50

THE TRAVELLER'S INTERNET GUIDE

**Edited by Jonathan Lorie
and Amy Sohanpaul**

A WEXAS publication

This first edition published in 2001
by WEXAS International
45-49 Brompton Road, London SW3 1DE, UK
telephone 020 7589 0500
fax 020 7589 8418
email mship@wexas.com
website www.wexas.com
© WEXAS International and authors 2001

ISBN 0-905-802-13-6

Cover design by Wylie Design, London
Printed and bound by Legoprint SpA, Italy

Cover pictures: Stone Images; Telegraph Colour
Library; Gyro Photography/Photonica

Contents ❧

Introduction ❧

T HE INTERNET IS DEAD.

That's what people said when the 'dotcom' bubble burst. But researching this book has revealed that the virtual world lives on. The dotcom shares may rise and fall, but cyberspace still offers a galaxy of information for the traveller.

We've sifted the heavenly multitude of websites and selected more than 1,000 of the best. What we've chosen are not the functional booking sites, but the less widely-known information sites, that put you in touch with people and places and – crucially – knowledge for your travels.

Here you'll find practical websites for every country in the world. That includes the confidently named Germany Wunderbar, the wishful Always Dreaming Of Bermuda, and the seductive Bali Paradise Online. If you're in the mood for a city break, we have Virtual Venice or Tokyo Meltdown. And for those who fancy a swim in the Baltic, there's Riga In Your Pocket.

For gastronomes we have a food section that includes Eat Germany and the World Sushi Guide. For adventurers there is Mountain Woman, there are Aquatic Outfitters, you might even be a Gear Head. Weathermen can check Hurricane Watch, the Snow And Avalanche Centre or, more simply, Rain Or Shine. Worriers can visit Virtual Hospital or Real World Rescue. Explorers can seek Maps Worldwide. And, in case you hadn't heard, there are Street Scams Of Barcelona.

Then we have such curiosities as The Divine Digest ('the electronic guide to world religions'); Shamash's Kosher Restaurant Database; and the ever-optimistic Indian Railways website.

The names are fun but the contents are genuinely fascinating. Best of all are the sites that put you in touch with people across the globe. That might be Locals In The Know or the Database Of Travel Helpers. It might be Peter's (I Live Here) Guide. Or it might just be Don and Linda Freedman, retirees from Toronto who are your hosts for adventure on their very own Travelzine.

Yes, the web is a weird and wonderful world. And it has a site for every one of us. ❧

Chapter 1: **Introducing the internet** ❧

by Chris Martin

RESEARCHING ON THE NET

BELIEVE IT OR NOT, everything you need to plan any kind of trip can already be found online. The internet today contains nearly one billion websites, a huge total to which hundreds more are added daily. The challenge for the web user is how to find the information they want quickly and accurately.

Recommendations from friends or web magazines will only go so far to help you. For the most part you will be on your own. The easiest way to navigate your way through this mass of information is by using an internet search engine. A search engine is essentially a website itself, but one which searches a database of other websites. A user simply logs on and enters a couple of relevant words into a search box. The site will then search its database and return a list of web pages which it thinks fit the query.

Not all search sites work in the same way, however. There are directory sites where human editors manually review websites and load them in to a hierarchical index system. Then there are search engines, which compile their databases using roving programs called 'robots' or 'spiders'. And Metasearch sites, which search a selection of sources including other search engines, encyclopaedias, news services and their own editorial content.

Directory sites

Directory-based sites, such as Yahoo (www.yahoo.com), tend to be the best kick-off point for beginners and general research. Though you can enter terms into a search box should you wish, you can also jump down the hierarchy of its database more directly. The websites are carefully arranged into a tree several layers deep and clearly marked with subheadings. You may even find that the site listings carry short reviews added by the publishers or lifted from each website's own metatags.

However, because directory sites are dependent on the human editors who maintain them, they are likely to contain fewer entries than their automated comrades. What's more, the manual process on which they depend means that entries may be out of date or incorrectly catalogued.

Search engines

A robot-based search engine like Altavista (www.altavista.com) is dependent largely on the information provided by the websites themselves. Primarily this comes from keywords included by the site's publishers within hidden metatags in the HTML code that makes up the page. These sites may also trawl through the editorial content of web pages to pick up clues from the text itself. To give some idea of the scale of the task: Altavista's spiders trawl through over 10 million sites a day and claim to have a database of over 200 million entries.

When you enter a query into its search box, the site will take your query, apply it to its database and, by using a mathematical algorithm, list the sites which most closely match your request.

The sheer efficiency of these search engines is also their downside. It soon becomes apparent that they will search everything. This means that even a simple query will produce a list containing hundreds of websites.

Metasearch sites

Bearing in mind the limitations of systems to search the internet and the immense size of the task, it seemed inevitable that someone would create search engines which search other search engines. Called metasearch sites, these are the librarians of the internet. A good example is Dogpile (www.dogpile.com). They will search other search engines and Usenet directories as well as a selection of maps, news sources, encyclopaedias and even weather reports. They will even offer a choice of how you would like your results delivered; by relevance, by sources, and so forth.

How relevant all this extra information is to most queries is debatable. A user who is trying to book a hotel may find it frustrating to have to pick their way through so many sources while trying to get a simple answer to a simple question.

Making the most of searching

While most of us will eventually settle on a couple of search sites with which we feel confident, there are two keys to successful searching, and you may find these helpful.

The first is to use the right site for your particular query. Let's say that you wish to find the website for a major airline. A large corporate company will, almost certainly, be listed in a *directory* site, so start with a directory site like Yahoo. Here you can either drill down through the hierarchy to 'Airlines' or simply enter 'British Airways' into its search box.

Now let us say you have booked an early flight, so you need to stay the night near the airport. A directory site will contain a random list of thousands of hotels, so you need to use the power of a proper *search engine,* such as Altavista. Now you can enter 'hilton hotel gatwick' to get results.

Finally, if you are just interested in airports for some reason and want to know everything about them, then it makes sense to use a *metasearch engine* such as Dogpile.

The second key is to attempt wherever possible to be 100 per cent clear in your enquiry, when you perform a search. Even the best search site can only use the wording that you give it, so vague or curt queries will result in disappointment or, more often, a huge and overwhelming result list.

A few tips

'Help': You can save yourself lots of time and effort when you arrive at a new search site by reading its help pages.

Boolean searching: Advanced users will be able to refine their query by using the Boolean system. Invented by mathematician George Boole over 100 years ago, it is a system of logical expressions which (in layman's terms) allows you to say 'and', 'only' and 'but not' in a way that the database understands.

Quotation marks: Framing your query in quotation marks will cause any search site to treat the words between them as a single phrase. For example "the big apple" will return information about New York rather than about large fruit.

Wildcard searching: The * symbol is read by a database to mean everything. To find a placename whose spelling you are unsure of, use a wildcard search. For example, instead of putting New Guinea, you could try *New G*.

Fastest search: The fastest search site is the text-only site Google (www.google.com).

Finding pictures: Some sites will take your query and search specifically for pictures, returning a page of thumbnail images rather than a list of links: for example Lycos (www.multimedia. lycos.com).

Capitals: Most search engines will assume that a query written in capitals is a placename.

Link Lists

On discovering a useful website, your next step should be to browse through its link list. Link lists form an exciting jumping-off point. For a start they have been compiled by people who share an interest and knowledge of the subject that you are researching. Effectively, they've done the work for you. Secondly, the site's owners will have selected sites of some worth, rather than ones which are outdated or are not very good. ❧

BUYING ON THE NET

THE INTERNET OFFERS A WEALTH of purchasing opportunities for the traveller. The relative ease with which companies – from huge international airlines to backroom bucket shops – can get online and publish information, means that there are thousands of companies offering their services online at any one time. What's more, you can access them 24 hours a day, 365 days a year.

Sometimes you will come across bargain offers being advertised that turn out to be window dressing, just as you would in the travel pages of any newspaper. But such inconveniences are far outweighed by what the internet can offer. In general, as websites are a good deal cheaper to run than a high street shop, savings in administrative costs can be passed on to the customer. Also, you can browse dozens of different travel agencies and offers without leaving the comfort of your living room.

The internet has direct access to the databases used by the travel agencies themselves (for example Travelocity at www.travelocity.co.uk uses SABRE), so the information about price and availability on sites should be bang up to date.

Look out, too, for the really clever stuff. Some sites will allow you not only to purchase but also to browse and choose the individual aeroplane seat of your choice, or to check ahead of time the comprehensive details of the hotel room you are booking. On top of all that, you have worldwide weather reports at your fingertips, and you can even use cameras ('webcams') to take a look at your destination live.

The only spanner in the works is actually paying for things. When it comes to handing over their hard-earned cash, many internet users are still nervous about online payment systems.

While there is nothing to stop you from using the internet as a glorified telephone directory of travel agents, the purpose of this chapter is to explain how internet security works and – hopefully – to put your mind at rest about using your credit card to purchase tickets and packages online.

Is it safe to use my credit card online?

Simply, the answer is 'yes'. Somehow a myth has circulated that faceless hackers can intercept the financial information which you give to a website and use it to empty your bank account.

The truth is that the internet is one of the safest places anywhere to use your credit card – a fact confirmed by both Visa and MasterCard. Secure internet systems have always been vastly safer than handing over your card to a stranger in a shop or over the telephone.

How is my credit card protected online?

The core of internet security is based around two software applications, both of which are run at server side (this means by the e-commerce company's computer which handles the transaction) and verified by your browser.

The first application is the Secure Sockets Layer (SSL). This is a military-strength encryption technology, which acts in conjunction with secure servers. It means that your credit card number is scrambled and encrypted with a code before being passed by a merchant server between your PC and that of the company taking your money. You can tell whether you are in a secure environment by the appearance of a little padlock in the bottom bar of your browser. It's simple. If the padlock is shut then SSL is running and you are perfectly safe to proceed.

The second application is a system of Digital Certificates. When your browser comes across a site that has a shopping system, it will automatically request to see that site's certificate. The certificate acts like an ID card for the site and the company behind it. It confirms their identity as the registered trader they claim to be. If the certificate does not belong to the site's registered owners, or is out of date, then your browser will display a screen warning you of this, or even stop you from continuing with the transaction. The warning screen itself will contain links to pages that explain the problem with the site's certificate and where to check up further on the site's owners.

What else can I do to protect myself?

It is best to exercise a little common sense when shopping online. If your SSL padlock is not closed, or if you receive a warning about a site's certificate, then definitely don't part with your credit card number.

When dealing with high street companies or big name airlines, obviously you have their existing reputation to make your decision by. However, newer web-based companies may be offering better deals but won't have been running long enough to build up a reputation. These sites are a shot in the dark, but if you are unsure about one, take a look in their 'About Us' section. There should be a trading address, current telephone and fax number and an email address. Call the company up and see how professional they sound, before you miss out on a bargain.

Always keep copies of your digital 'paper trail' when you are purchasing online. You can do this by hitting your browser's print button to make a hard copy of the various screens that list and confirm what you have purchased. You should also print out any email confirmations you get sent. This is such a simple precaution that it's easy to forget to do. However, not doing it is the equivalent of throwing your travel documents and credit card stubs in the bin. Should you need to complain at a later date, or sort out an administrative mistake, these details will be invaluable.

What is the industry doing to help?

The majority of your statutory rights apply just as much online as they do in the high street.

Travel agents are likely to be bonded by one or more of the larger consumer agencies such as ABTA (Association of British Travel Agents) (www.abta.com). Anyone selling airline tickets in the UK also needs an ATOL license (Air Travel Organiser's Licence) (www.atol.org.uk). Both qualifications are set up to ensure that you do not get stranded at your destination and that you have some recourse to get your money refunded should the firm go bust. (See the section 'Consumer issues' in Chapter 3.)

The European Union also offers protection to citizens of its member states, which apply to travel agents on- and offline. These initiatives normally cover serious stuff such as insolvency. To qualify for protection here, you will have to have been sold an all-inclusive package. This means a trip that runs for longer than a 24-hour duration and involves more than one form of transport, accommodation or tourist service.

The internet itself is trying to tidy up its act. Look out for industry watchdogs who run logo schemes. For example, the UK-based consumer magazine *Which?* runs the Which? Web Trader scheme. The scheme asserts rigid rules of conduct on e-commerce sites before allowing them to display their logo. The sites are also tested and checked by the scheme's representatives. ❧

COMMUNICATING ON THE NET

Once you have got used to moving around the internet, and can search for and access information easily, you will have at your fingertips the world's greatest library. There are millions of pages of information on every topic under the sun to read and digest. However, the real joy of the cyberworld lies not just in its physical resources but its human ones.

The internet at its core is all about communication. Everywhere you turn you are encouraged to get in touch, offer your opinion or pitch in on a debate. At the very centre of all this internet communication is email.

Email

More than flashy websites, bargain offers, or up-to-date information, new internet users cite access to email (Electronic Mail) as their primary reason for going online. Email is a fast and efficient way of sending text messages between internet users. The system is instant, global and free. What's more, you can use it to send pictures, sound files and documents as 'attachments' – files which piggyback on an email and are then saved and opened on the recipient's hard drive.

What's in a name?

You don't need to own a website to get an email address, as you can share the domain name of your ISP (Internet Service Provider). Email is hosted for individuals or companies by an ISP, who can set up an email account and even give you a unique domain name. These unique domain names mean that you can find out a good deal about someone from their email address.

Let's take for example 'jthompson@travelbook.co.uk'. The email address is divided into two pieces by the '@' (meaning 'at'). The first half of the address gives information about the user, while the second half shows information about the server that hosts their account.

The first piece of information tells us that the user is called 'jthompson' and tells the server to drop the message into his mail box.

The second piece of information comes in three sections. The first, 'travelbook', is the name of the ISP. The second part, 'co', tells us that we are dealing with a commercial company. The third, 'uk', tells us that the user is based in the UK.

You can find lists of the various acronyms used in domain names online, though these tend to be straightforward; for example 'vichy.ac.fr' would be a French, academic institution.

Collecting your email

You will need to get hold of some specialist software with which to send and read email, called an email client. The most popular ones are Eudora, Outlook Express and Netscape Messenger (which is incorporated into the Netscape browser).

To configure an email client to connect to your ISP's email server, you will need to know various details about your account. The address of its SMTP (Simple Message Transfer Protocol) server to send email and the address of it's POP3 server to receive email. You will also need your user name and password to get past the server's security. Most of these are set up automatically when you initially install the internet software supplied by your ISP, using a set-up wizard. But it is worth keeping a note of these settings should you need to install a new client or configure a different computer.

The email client allows you to organise your sent, received and draft email into folders. It can also keep an address book of your regularly used email addresses, handle a mailing list, and download your email to read offline at your leisure; hence saving money on your phone bill. Most email clients will even help with your spelling and grammar, acting like a word processor.

Email has a language all of its own. Experienced email users will speed up the typing process by using abbreviations and even graphical short-cuts called 'emoticons'. It's great fun to learn but does not mean that the rules of spelling and grammar are entirely ignored. No one will be upset with you for using the spellcheck before firing off a mail.

Email on the move

One of the most exciting developments in online communications has been the birth of web-based email. Web-based email functions in exactly the same way as conventional email, allowing you to send, receive and store email and attachments. But a web-based email account, such as Hotmail (www.hotmail. com), is hosted on a web server and can be accessed and set up via a web site. Not only does this mean that web-based email accounts can be set up quickly and conveniently online, but it also means that they can be accessed from any computer with an internet connection, anywhere in the world.

A traveller running a web-based email account can pick up his mail from a hotel, a library or even a cybercafé. Web-based email is a traveller's dream, allowing people on the road to keep in touch with home or their fellow travellers without depending on pricey telephone calls, or finding themselves at the mercy of mail drops and international time zones. ❧

Chapter 2: **Where are you going?** ❧

by Amy Sohanpaul

DESTINATIONS WORLDWIDE

Websites for every country are listed below, arranged in alphabetical order. For guidebooks and travel articles on various destinations, see Chapter 3 – 'Books', 'Travel Journalism', 'Travelogues and Chatsites'. But first, here are some useful sites covering the whole world or entire regions.

GLOBAL SITES

WEXAS

www.wexas.com
A one-stop resource centre for all kinds of travel, this site has a library of destination guides from Lonely Planet and the Rough Guides series, plus 'The Traveller's Handbook' (which has a profile for every country) and the Columbus World Travel Guide – the travel agent's bible. Also contains an online version of 'The Traveller's Internet Guide' with updates, and extensive trip-planning facilities. Produced by WEXAS, the club for independent travellers.

About.com – Travel

http://home.about.com/travel/index.html
Part of a network of over 700 sites, this is a comprehensive directory with good background and practical information on most travel destinations. Countries, continents, culture and language – About.com's experts have selected the best sites for each category.

CIA World Factbook

www.odci.gov/cia/publications/factbook
Country profiles in thorough detail from the Central Intelligence Agency – everything from political background and geographic coordinates to economy overviews. Click on Chiefs of State for details on leadership in foreign countries. Heavy-duty information.

World Travel Guide.net

www.travel-guides.com
From Columbus , who publish the 'World Travel Guide', an invaluable reference for travel professionals: detailed data on countries.

The Royal Commonwealth Society

www.rcsint.org
The RCS has a Commonwealth-wide network of societies and branches, and this site is a good starting point if you're thinking of becoming a member. Numerous social and cultural events, talks and exhibitions provide an insider's view of the member nations. They publish the most interesting talks online.

Database of Travel Helpers

www.geocities.com/TheTropics/2442/database.html
What is the telephone number of that hotel in Acapulco? Which is the most popular credit card in Turkey? Someone on this site should know – it's a network of people ready to answer questions about the areas they live in or have travelled extensively in.

Rec.Travel Library

www.travel-library.com
An interesting assortment of personal travelogues, travel stories and trip reports as well as handy tips on safety and scams, packing and worldwide travel information with links for any destination. Practical sections include detailed advice for Round-the-World trips, and links to the CIA World Factbook for country statistics and Tourism Offices Worldwide.

World Heritage Cities

www.ovpm.org
This site looks at the 164 cities which include inhabited sites listed as cultural properties on UNESCO's World Heritage List, including Damascus, Lima and San Gimignano.

Official Travel Information

www.officialtravelinfo.com
Over 1000 official tourism organisations pool content on this site.

While it isn't truly a worldwide guide – clicking on the map of Africa brings up just four listings – it's still pretty extensive, and the areas that are covered are covered in detail.

Association of National Tourist Offices in the UK

www.antor.com
Contact details for tourist offices in the UK, with good links for more information on the destinations represented.

Tourism Offices Worldwide Directory

www.towd.com
An extensive directory of local tourist information sources. Covers most destinations, and only lists official government tourism offices, convention and visitors bureaus, chambers of commerce and other agencies providing accurate travel and free information.

Local Times Around the World

www.hilink.com.au/times
Will it be dark when you get there? Click on this site and find out local lighting-up times around the world.

International Airports

www.gsa-scandinavia.dk/airport.htm
Links to airport homepages worldwide.

BBC World Service

www.bbc.co.uk/worldservice
News, features and reports from around the world.

Local Newspapers

www.thepaperboy.com *and* www.onlinenewspapers.com *and* www.newsdirectory.com
These sites provide links to newspapers around the world.

World Information

www.worldinformation.com
Simply click on the map for business, political and economic information on every country. Excellent resource.

AFRICA: REGIONAL SITES

A Brief Guide to Africa

www.africa.co.uk/country/af-guide.htm
Comparitive socio-economic profiles of African Countries. Very basic information.

AfriCam

www.africam.co.za
Instant visual essence of Africa. Offers more than pretty pictures – facts galore in their mammal, bird and reptile guides, there's even a spoor guide with information on tracking.

Africa Insites

www.africa-insites.com
Not all of Africa is covered by this site, but the in-depth travel guides to Zambia, Lesotho, Namibia and Uganda are packed with facts on everything from what time the borders open to what clothes to take. Beautiful photography.

Africa Online

www.africaonline.com
Claims not to be a 'cheesy zebra and sunsets site' and offers news, developments and discussions from all over Africa, as well as information about arts, culture and health. Does have travel-specific pages, with summaries outlining the main attractions.

Arab Net

www.arab.net
Covers North Africa and the Middle East, providing very detailed country-by-country data.

Lexic Orient

http://lexiorient.com
North Africa and the Middle East explored – all the latest news, as well as travel-specific and general reference information, complete with a learn Arabic online course.

New Africa

www.newafrica.com
Facts, figures, news and travel guides for most African countries.

ASIA: REGIONAL SITES

Accommodating Asia

www.accomasia.com
Annotated links to travel diaries, history, music, food and regional pages; and includes message boards.

Asia Links

www.gergo.com/pauline/asia/index.htm
All sorts of Asian information, from useful travel hints and culture to recipes and jokes. Covers China, Hong Kong, India, Indonesia, Japan, Korea, Malaysia, Singapore, Taiwan and Thailand.

Asia Tour

www.asiatour.com
A one-stop source for travel guides to almost every Asian country. Also includes news and feature articles.

Do Asia

www.doasia.com
Entertainment guide to major Asian cities from Bombay and Bangkok to Tokyo, including reviews of restaurants and bars.

CARIBBEAN: REGIONAL SITES

Do It Caribbean

www.doitcaribtourism.com/
Do it easily on this site: pick a topic, such as diving or eating out, or pick a destination, and you're virtually there.

French Caribbean

www.frenchcaribbean.com
Diving, sightseeing, eating, drinking and fun in the islands.

EUROPE: REGIONAL SITES

City Vox

www.cityvox.com
A tourist guide, events listings and local newspaper rolled into one, with information on eating out, exhibitions and sightseeing in major cities across Europe.

Visit Europe

www.visiteurope.com
Comprehensive site with fast facts and background information on most European countries. Also offers related links, which reveal further insights – the art of drinking beer in Belgium or a look at the Cannes Festival in France.

Europe Travel and Tourism Information

www.travel-library.com/europe
Travelogues and general information on European destinations. Also links to directories of Europe-related websites, such as BusWeb, the European bus service index.

Backpack Europe on a Budget

www.backpackeurope.com
Not just for backpackers – as well as some country-specific information, this site offers links to several useful pages, with tips for women travellers and on keeping in touch while abroad.

Freetodo

www.Freetodo.freeserve.co.uk
Free attractions in selected countries in Europe.

In Your Pocket

www.inyourpocket.com
Portal to a series of travel guides with comprehensive coverage of Eastern and Central Europe.

LATIN AMERICA: REGIONAL SITES

Latin American Travel Association

www.lata.org
Country-by-country round-ups including visa, health, climate.

Latin America

www.latinamericatraveler.com
Travel news, security reports, and addresses for Spanish schools.

South America for Visitors

www.gosouthamerica.about.com
Extensive site. Click on 'Travel Planning' for practical tips, summarised destination reports, top attractions and country listings.

Travel Latin America

www.travellatinamerica.com
Mixed bag of practical information: national holidays, business contacts, visas, weather, travel articles, book and film reviews.

MIDDLE EAST: REGIONAL SITES

Arab Net

www.arab.net
Owned by publishers of Saudi's leading papers. Covers the Middle East and North Africa with detailed country-by-country data.

Lexic Orient

http://lexiorient.com
All the latest news, as well as travel-specific and general reference information, complete with a learn Arabic online course.

PACIFIC: REGIONAL SITES

South Pacific Islands Travel Channel

www.pi-travel.com
Click on the map for information on any of the islands.

SITES FOR EACH COUNTRY

(See also 'Dependent Territories' on page 134.)

AFGHANISTAN

Afghanistan Online

www.afghan-web.com
Everything you ever wanted to know about Afghanistan – from general facts to news, culture, history, to a photogallery and a thought-provoking section on 'The Plight of the Afghan Woman'.

ALBANIA

Albania – Land of the Eagles

www.albania.co.uk
Albanian news and information, and potted city guides outlining the main attractions.

ALGERIA

Mifta Shamali - Algeria

www.i-cias.com/m.s/algeria
This site acknowledges that travelling is difficult and restricted but offers tips on health, safety, food and where to stay.

ANDORRA

Andorra, The Pyrenean Country

www.turisme.ad/index.html
Where to go, what to do and how to relax in Andorra.

ANGOLA

Ministry of Tourism

www.angola.org/
The official site, with an emphasis on current news, investment,

reconstruction and trade. Gives a round-up of geography, climate and the different provinces and also looks at art and culture.

ANTARCTICA

British Antarctic Survey

www.antarctica.ac.uk
The emphasis is on the scientific here, with lists of geological and physical science resources, relevant news stories and mapping and geographic information, but the 'About Antarctica' section gives a detailed picture of the continent for general travellers.

Virtual Antarctica

www.terraquest.com/antarctica
Online account of an expedition to Antarctica, recounted in the ship's log and in pictures, plus information about the history of the continent, its environment, a guidebook with an Antarctic glossary, a checklist of wildlife and an Antarctic reading list.

Lonely Planet – Destination Antarctica

www.lonelyplanet.com/dest/ant/ant.htm
The most isolated, least explored continent in the world, but this site makes it as accessible as possible for travellers.

ANTIGUA & BARBUDA

Antigua & Barbuda – Official Travel Guide

www.antigua-barbuda.org
Information-packed official homepage of the Department of Tourism, covering everything from history to culture, travel tips to a calender of events. It's cricket, beaches and carnival all the way.

ARGENTINA

Argentour.com

www.argentour.com
Sponsored by the the Argentinian Embassy in Norway, this site

gives a good overview, through text, pictures and videos, of all things Argentinian, from the history, weather, news, economy, geography and people to the tango, with potted biographies of the main tango musicians and singers.

República Argentina – Secretaría de Turismo

www.sectur.gov.ar/homepage.htm
The National Tourist Board's site is a good starting point for visitors. General information includes when to go and what clothes to pack, internal transport, and some social background. Click onto 'Argentina Tour' for detailed information on different regions from the Great Waters Rainforest to La Pampa and the Patagonian Andes to the Patagonian Atlantic.

ARMENIA

All About Armenia

www.tourismarmenia.com
The Tourist Information Centre's site, with historical and cultural background, a photo gallery, and practical tips for travellers.

AUSTRALIA

Australia.com

www.global.australia.com *and* www.australia.com
The official site of the Australian Tourist Commission, with information on Australian cities, beaches, reefs, outback, wildlife, and lifestyle. Includes handy traveller's resource and travel tips.

About Australia

www.about-australia.com
Information on each state, including places to see, travel tips, local transport, events, culture, education and health.

The Aussie Traveller

www.wilmap.com.au
Information, maps and photographs for Australian towns, links to

Government departments, touring ideas, national parks, muse-ums, galleries and good links.

Travel Australia

www.travelaustralia.com.au
Click on a region on the map for attractions and accommodation.

Australian Capital Territory

Australia's National Capital

www.canberratourism.com.au
Official tourist information site, with details on all the attractions Canberra has to offer, including art galleries, restaurants, enter-tainment, sports and shopping.

New South Wales

Tourism New South Wales

www.tourism.nsw.gov.au
Sydney, the South Coast and every other attraction in New South Wales are explored in detail on this official tourism site.

Sydney Sidewalk

www.sydney.sidewalk.com.au
What's on in Sydney – events, clubs, pubs and other places to go.

Sydney Airport

www.acay.com.au/~willt/yssy/
Airport services, transportation, tourist tips, food and shopping at Sydney Airport.

Sapphire Coast Tourism

www.sapphirecoast.com.au
A site devoted to the beautiful South Coast region with maps, travel tips, events calender and information on whale watching.

Northern Territory

Autralia's Northern Territory

www.nttc.com.au
The 'Travel Information' and 'Must See' sections have all the information needed for a visit to the 'real Outback' state.

Alice Springs Airport

www.aliceairport.com.au
Flight schedules, car parking and airport services.

Queensland

Destination Queensland

www.queensland-holidays.com.au
Queensland is full of diverse attractions ranging from the city-chic of Brisbane to lush forests and long beaches, and this site looks at them all.

Brisbane International Airport

www.bne.com.au
Airport information, and a visitors' guide to Brisbane, the Gold Coast, Moreton Bay and other destinations in Queensland.

South Australia

South Australia Tourism Commission

www.southaustralia.com
All the necessary facts for visiting Adelaide and South Australia.

Tasmania

Discover Tasmania

www.discovertasmania.com.au
Stylish, succinct and useful site, outlining what to do and see in Tasmania.

Western Australia

Western Australian Tourism Commission

www.westernaustralia.net

Western Australia spans over 2.5 million square km (1 million square miles) and is arguably the largest state in the world. This site condenses it to a managable size, with fast facts and handy travel tips.

Perth International Airport

www.perthairport.net.au

Well-presented information about the airport and its services, with additional links to related sites.

Victoria

Tourism Victoria

www.visitvictoria.com

Cities, towns, places of interest and getting around in Victoria.

Melbourne Visitors Guide

www.melbourne.8m.com

Practical guide with good links and travel tips.

AUSTRIA

Austrian National Tourist Office

www.austria-tourism.at

Basic background information, and some interesting facts and figures, including the water temperature in Austrian lakes.

Vienna Online

www.magwien.gv.at/english

All the facts about all the attractions, from the famous Spanish Riding School to the Vienna Teddy Bear Museum and the Vienna Vampire Museum.

Vienna International Airport

www.viennaairport.com/englisch/
Flight information, local transport links and airport cafés, bars and restaurants.

AZERBAIJAN

A-Z of Azerbaijan

www.azerb.com
A complete source of information on Azerbaijan. Click on the lengthy list, which includes bookshops, embassies, food, fauna and flora; or the map to find out more about different regions.

BAHAMAS

The Islands of the Bahamas

www.bahamas.com
Choose an island or experience from the drop-down menu for details on activities, accommodation, an events calendar, and an 'Island Guide' which covers everything else.

BAHRAIN

Bahrain Tourism

www.bahraintourism.com
State-sponsored site, an efficient round-up of the main attractions and tips for travellers.

Bahrain International Airport

www.bahrainairport.com
Airport facilities and passenger services at Bahrain International, a major air hub for the Gulf region.

BANGLADESH

Virtual Bangladesh

www.virtualbangladesh.com

A wide-ranging and interesting site, with news pages, live chats and discussion forums; and of specific interest to travellers, a section called 'The Grand Tour', full of vital statistics, notes on culture and lifestyle, a visitor's guide and an English to Bengali dictionary.

BARBADOS

Barbados Tourism Encyclopedia

www.barbados.org
The official Barbados Tourism Authority site. Travel information, maps, events and a picture gallery.

BELARUS

WWW Belarus

www.belarus.net
Pitched at business people, but this site includes some information on news and culture and includes a (very) basic section on travel, and some links to resources in Belarus.

BELGIUM

Living in Belgium

www.expatica.com/belgium.asp
Primarily for expatriates in Belgium but the menu on the left reveals information about what's on in Belgium and information on travel and transport.

Ardenne-Brussels

www.belgium-tourism.net
Art, music and museums in Brussels, châteaux, historic residences and outdoor activities in the Ardennes; general data for both.

Tourist Office for Flanders

www.visitflanders.com
Things to do and see along the Flemish coast and in the 'art cities' of Brussels, Bruges, Antwerp, Ghent, Mechelen and Leuven.

Artsite Belgium Homepage

www.artsite.be
A virtual art guide to galleries, museums and auction houses in Belgium.

Brussels Airport/Brussels Charleroi Airport

www.brusselsairport.be *and* www.charleroi-airport.com
Information on Brussel's two major airports.

BELIZE

Belize!

www.travelbelize.org
This official site from the Belize Tourism Board is well laid out and helpful, with advice on when to travel and what to pack, things to do and places to see; and general background information on the history and culture of the island.

Belize Online

www.belize.com
A tourism and investment guide from Belize First magazine.

BENIN

Destination Benin

www.lonelyplanet.com/destinations/africa/benin/
Facts for the traveller, when to go, attractions, culture, environment, getting around and background data from Lonely Planet.

BERMUDA

Always Dreaming Of Bermuda

www.dreamingofbermuda.bm
An exhaustive directory of links to virtually everything connected with Bermuda , including local newpapers, related books, music, restaurants, travelogues and photo galleries.

Bermuda International Airport

www.bermudaairport.com
Flight and passenger information and facilities at Bermuda International.

BHUTAN

The Kingdom of Bhutan

www.kingdomofbhutan.com
Rich in information, this official site provides background information on the history, people and culture of Bhutan, and explores traditional arts and sports, food and festivals in the Visitor Information section.

BOLIVIA

Bolivia Web

www.boliviaweb.com
A comprehensive resource: information on history, regions, food, national parks, plus links to books, travelogues and photogalleries.

BOSNIA & HERZEGOVINA

Destination Bosnia-Hercegovina

www.lonelyplanet.com/destinations/europe/
bosnia-hercegovina
The few sites that are related to Bosnia-Hercegovina are personal travelogues. This offering from Lonely Planet offers factual detail and advice on travelling in this sensitive area.

BOTSWANA

Republic of Botswana

www.gov.bw/
Click on the 'Tourism' section of this official government site for a breakdown of attractions, national parks, where to stay, internal transport, and information on visas, currency, and health.

BRAZIL

Brazilian Embassy in London

www.brazil.org.uk
This is also the site for the Brazilian tourist board, so the information available is useful for both general and business travellers, covering economy and politics, culture and travel advice.

Brazil Info – Your Guide to Brazil

www.brazilinfo.com
General information about Brazil, as well as a hotel directory, descriptions of the national parks and a photo gallery.

All About Rio

www.ipanema.com
Rio for beginners, Rio for old hands – there's a mix of both basic and detailed information on this site.

Rio de Janiero International Airport

www.aviationbr.com/gig/
Most of the pages on this site are under construction, but when finished it promises to provide maps, details of services and a guide to Rio de Janeiro.

BRUNEI

Brunei Darussalam Homepage

www.brunet.bn
The tourism section of this site has some useful tips on customs and traditions in Brunei, basic information on tourist attractions, and a list of restaurants and shops.

BULGARIA

Travel Bulgaria

www.travel-bulgaria.com
History, traditions, festivals, culture and cuisine are outlined on

this site, with additional information on passports and visas, currency and the climate.

Sofia Airport

www.sofia-airport.bg
Arrival and departure information, and an atlas of Sofia.

BURKINA FASO

Excite Travel Destinations: Burkina Faso

www.excite.com/travel/countries/burkina_faso/
Concise but comprehensive information on visiting Burkina Faso, with great advice in the 'do and don't' section.

BURUNDI

Destination Burundi

www.lonleyplanet.com/destinations/africa/burundi/index.htm
Not exactly a travel guide, more a destination warning. Provides links to Information Burundi and the International Crisis Group for more details on the civil conflict in the country.

CAMBODIA

Cambodia-Web

www.cambodia-web.net
Some pages are being redesigned, but 'Fine Arts' and 'Travel Tales' give a flavour of the Kingdom of Cambodia.

CAMEROON

Postcards from Cameroon

www.geocities.com/TheTropics/Shores/4051
Click on the map or the cities index for regional reviews. These are personal pages created by a Cameroonian, and informal in style and content but provide an insider's overview.

CANADA

Travel Canada

www.travelcanada.ca/travelcanada/eng/index.cfm
The official site of the Canadian Tourism Commision. It is also an interactive state-of-the-art site, overflowing with practical and inspiring information about Canada.

Out There

www.out-there.com
Full of information about the great outdoors in Canada – parks, mountains, lakes – and what to do in all that wilderness.

Ski Guide

www.ski-guide.com
A guide to all the skiing and snowboarding resorts in Canada and the USA.

Alberta

Discover Alberta

www.discoveralberta.com
Interactive maps, photo galleries and introductory articles combine to give a detailed picture of this state, from the Rocky Mountains to the cities of Calgary and Edmonton.

British Colombia

British Colombia World Web Travel Guide

www.bc.worldweb.com/
Featuring trip planning, useful links, a guide to Vancouver and ski resorts, events and entertainment, this site also has a photo gallery and webcams to make the picture complete.

Vancouver International Airport

www.yvr.ca
Detailed guides of the airport layout, flight information, food,

transportation, parking, services, facilities, shopping – this airport site packs in as much detail as many city sites.

Manitoba

Travel Manitoba

www.travelmanitoba.com
Quick facts, an events guide and basic visitor information.

New Brunswick

The Official New Brunswick Website

www.tourismnbcanada.com/web/
Click on 'About NB' in the left hand index for anwers to frequently asked questions, general travel information, snowmobiling regulations and facts about New Brunswick.

Newfoundland & Labrador

Newfoundland and Labrador Tourism

www.gov.nf.ca/tourism/
Clear site, easy to navigate and beautifully illustrated. Everything a visitor would need, including avoiding moose on the motorway.

Northwest Territories

NWT Explorers' Guide

www.nwttravel.nt.ca
Three drop-down menus contain information related to listings and services, features and interests, and regional maps and guides.

Nova Scotia

Explore Nova Scotia

http://explore.gov.ns.ca/
The official tourism website, a useful round-up of all the attractions of this coastal state.

Nunavut

Find out about Nunavut

www.nunatour.nt.ca
An easy-to-navigate overview of this remote region.

The Nunavut Handbook

www.arctic-travel.com
*Possibly the most comprehensive travel guide to Canada's Arctic –
although it doesn't appear to have been updated since April 2000,
the regional descriptions are detailed and still relevant.*

Ontario

About Ontario

www.travelinx.com/ont_mn.html
*Wide-ranging facts and figures for the visitor, from the history of
Ontario's coat of arms to emergency services.*

Info Niagara

www.infoniagara.com
*Six sections on this site highlight all the attractions and diversity of
the Niagara Region.*

Lester B. Pearson International Airport

www.lbpia.toronto.on.ca
*Information about the airport, the Greater Toronto Airports Au-
thority, destinations, flights, shopping and services*

Prince Edward Island

Tourism Prince Edward Island

www.peiplay.com
*The official guide to visiting the island, including things to do.
Travel Essentials gives details of the six touring regions, informa-
tion centres and maps.*

Québec

Tourisme Québec

www.bonjour-quebec.com
An inviting and informative site – all the city's fun, including a delightful description of the ancient ritual of 'Sugaring Off'.

Aéroports de Montréal

www.admtl.com
As it says.

Saskatchewan

Tourism Saskatchewan

www.sasktourism.com
Energetic, enthusiastic site – you have to dodge the exclamation marks for information on where to go and what to do.

Yukon Territory

Tourism Yukon

www.touryukon.com
Untouched wilderness and wildlife on a grand scale add to the attraction of this remote state, fully explored on this official site.

CAPE VERDE

A Travel Guide to Cape Verde

www.newafrica.com/travelguides/capeverde.htm
A quick look at the islands, with details on essentials like vaccinations, climate and currency.

CENTRAL AFRICAN REPUBLIC

Destination Central African Republic

www.lonelyplanet.com/destinations/africa/central_african_republic/

In amongst the descriptions of lush national parks, there is a strong warning on visits to this fascinating but dangerous country.

CHAD

Destination Chad

www.lonelyplanet.com.au/dest/afr/cha.htm
Dependable destinational information from Lonely Planet.

CHILE

Go Chile!

www.gochile.cl
Bang up to date, but some pages are in Spanish, due to be translated soon. Enough information in English to get a flavour of Chile.

CHINA

China Daily

www.chinadaily.com.cn/
Check out the news about China as read in China. Also offers a language tips section.

China on Internet

www.chinaoninternet.com/
Follow the 'Travel in China' link to various regions, or take a look at Chinese movies, traditional operas and the art of kung fu. Links to sites on Shanghai, Shandong and Nanjing.

China Today

www.chinatoday.com/
Heavy duty information on Chinese history, culture, tradition, law and justice, and city and province guides.

China Now

www.chinanow.com
The ultimate guide to city life in China, including Guangzhou,

Chengdu, Beijing, Shanghai, Nanjing and Kunming.

The Beijing Page

www.flashpaper.com/beijing
Background to Beijing in some detail – weather, attractions, museums, food, tourist diaries and a photo gallery.

Shanghai City Guide

www.worldexecutive.com/cityguides/shanghai
Restaurants, attractions, weather, photographs and good travel tips – including currency, tipping, dress codes and etiquette.

That's Shanghai

www.thatsshanghai.com
All about going out and having a good time: listings for dining out, nightlife, stage, cinemas and art, as well as a travel section.

Welcome to Sichuan

www.scsti.ac.cn/En/tourism.html
Basic background information on the main attractions in this province, famous for its spicy cuisine.

Discover Hong Kong

www.hkta.org
Lively site from the Tourist Association. Facts, festivals, culture, dining, tips for mature travellers, and a very useful events section.

Hong Kong

www.english.hongkong.com
Finance, business, technology, sport, entertainment... and a great travel section, with a guide to speaking Cantonese and articles, features and a photo gallery.

Hong Kong International Airport

www.hkid.com/people/hkg/
The 'HKG Site Index' box allows for searches by topic: clicking on the 'News' navigation box brings up tourist attractions.

Macau

Macau Government Tourist Office

www.macautourism.gov.mo
Travel information on all the attractions Macau has to offer, from the Dragon Boat Festival to women's volleyball matches.

COLOMBIA

Colombia Tourism Page

www.drcomputer.com/colombia/guide01.htm
The pages on the Caribbean and Amazonian regions are currently under construction, but the rest of this site gives detailed background information and plenty of details on the Andean regions.

Peter's (I Live Here) Guide to Colombia

www.poorbuthappy.com/colombia/
Frank, fearless and fair take on life in Colombia. In-depth articles give advice to travellers – what to do/not to do, where to go/avoid, and there's a commonsense guide to common scams. The advice on being kidnapped could be more detailed: 'If you are kidnapped you are in big trouble so avoid being kidnapped.'

COMORO ISLANDS

The Comoro Islands' Home Page

www.ksu.edu/sasw/comoros/comoros.html
Sometimes known as The Forgotten Islands, the Comoros are home to rare species, wonderful beaches and a fascinating maritime history, all covered on this site.

CONGO (BRAZZAVILLE)

A Travel Guide to Congo

www.newafrica.com/travelguides/congo.htm
Basic background details, including information on internal travel, essential documentation and recommended immunisations.

CONGO (DEMOCRATIC REPUBLIC)

The World Factbook – Democratic Republic of Congo

www.cia.gov/cia/publications/factbook/geos/cg.html
This page from 'The World Factbook' delivers a view of the country as seen by the men in black. Statistics, facts, figures – the state of the nation.

COOK ISLANDS

Cook Islands Tourism Corporation

www.cook-islands.com
Another official gateway to paradise. Detailed information on how to get there, what to do on arrival, from horseriding right down to aerobics classes.

COSTA RICA

Info Costa Rica.com

www.infocostarica.com
'Articles in General' looks at festivals, safety, health and travelling in Costa Rica, the 'Cool Stuff' folder contains maps and a photo gallery as well as Spanish lessons.

Tourism Costa Rica!

www.tourism-costarica.com
Costa Rica covers 0.03% of the world's surface yet contains about 6% of its biodiversity. Other good reasons to visit are outlined in this official site, which has plenty of practical tips as well.

COTE D'IVOIRE

Cote d'Ivoire Travel Guide

www.newafrica.com/travelguides/cotedivoire.asp
The list on the left refers to information for all countries in Africa. Scroll down the page of brief but useful facts and click on 'A Profile of Cote d'Ivoire for further information.

CROATIA

Croatian National Tourist Board

www.htz.hr
An efficient and informative round-up of all the attractions that Croatia has to offer.

Zagreb Tourist Board

www.zagreb-convention.hr
The word 'zagreb' means a trench, according to this site, which is full of rich detail. Interactive maps provide information on the surrounding areas, while two virtual walks through the city take in the main attractions.

Greetings from Hvar

www.hvar.hr
Greetings from the Hvar Hygienic Society and travel information on Hvar Island on the Adriatic coast of Croatia.

Plitvice National Park

www.np-plitvice.tel.hr/np-plitvice
The park is beautiful enough to be on UNESCO's World Heritage List, and the site proves it through some stunning photographs alongside useful information for visitors.

CUBA

Cuban Culture

www.cubanculture.com
Curiosities and gems of information about Cuba and Cubans, good general background information and more detailed studies of the music, dance and art of Cuba.

CubaNet

www.cubanet.org
Site set up by Cuban exiles, providing a 'non-governmental version' of the events and daily life in Cuba, and links to related sites.

Granma Internacional

www.granma.cu/ingles/index.htm
The official newspaper of the Communist Party of Cuba.

CYPRUS

Cyprus Tourism Organisation

www.cyprustourism.org
Full of tips and temptations, details of regions to visit and a look at the incredible history of this island where Cleopatra holidayed.

CZECH REPUBLIC

Czech Tourism Pages

www.czech-tourism.com
A handy collection of links to all thing Czechoslovakian.

1st in Prague

www.praguetourist.com
Checklist of activities and attractions in Prague.

DENMARK

Visit Denmark

www.dt.dk
The Danish tourist board site, although a little fiddly to use, will match up areas with activities to find all related information.

Wonderful Copenhagen

www.woco.dk
Wonderfully detailed site. Clicking the index lists information on everything from activities to zoos, taking in the Tivoli gardens and Hans Christian Anderson on the way.

Copenhagen Airport

www.cph.dk
The low-down on Denmark's main air terminal.

Faroe Islands Tourist Guide

www.faroeislands.com
This evocative site gives plenty of reasons to tempt visitors to these islands halfway between Iceland and Norway.

DJIBOUTI

INFOHUB Djibouti Travel Guide

www.infohub.com/travelguide/traveller/africa/djibouti.html
Links to pages that provide basic information on Djibouti.

DOMINICA

Welcome to Dominica

www.dominica.dm
Boiling lakes, waterfalls, unspoiled rainforest, beaches – this site explores all the attractions of Dominica.

DOMINICAN REPUBLIC

Travel Facts – Dominican Republic

www.travelfacts.com/tfats/htm/dr/drdest.htm
Scroll down for the useful parts of this site – the headings from 'History' to 'Information', or 'Travel' for a destination overview.

ECUADOR

Ecuador Explorer

http://ecuadorexplorer.com
Country data and travel tips, immunisations and safety.

EGYPT

Egypt Voyager

www.egyptvoyager.com/
As well as travel tips and information on history, the pyramids,

museums and monuments, this excellent site carries interesting articles about Egyptian life and attractions.

Complete Online Guide to Alexandria

www.alex-guide.com
Ancient history, modern shopping, practical tips and a virtual guided tour that provides a snapshot of the main sites in this fashionable coastal resort.

Cairo

www.cairotourist.com
Information on all the attractions in Cairo, from the famous museums to the not-so-famous nightclubs.

EL SALVADOR

El Salvador

www.elsalvadorturismo.gob.sv
This site roams from volcanoes to archaelogical sites, from beaches and surfing to fishing.

EQUATORIAL GUINEA

Equatorial Guinea Page

www.sas.upenn.edu/African_Studies/Country_Specific/Eq_Guinea.html
Provides links to basic information about the country.

ERITREA

Eritrean Network Information Centre

www.eritrea.org
The latest news, basic facts and figures, regional information and travel tips.

Estonia

Estonian Tourist Board

www.tourism.ee
Regional information, events, and all aspects of trip preparation for a visit to this increasingly popular destination.

Tallinn

www.tallinn.ee/english/index.html
The essential facts and figures, and a good historical overview.

Ethiopia

Ethiopia The Land of Mystery

www.tourethio.com
Background and regional information on the oldest independent nation in Africa.

Fiji

Fiji Visitors Bureau

www.bulafiji.com
Follow the 'Fiji Is' link for a succession of stunning shots. The 'About Fiji' section provides more detailed, practical information.

Finland

Finnish Tourist Board

www.mek.fi
Jam-packed with useful information, this official site is the best starting point for travellers intending to visit Finland.

Virtual Finland

http://virtual.finland.fi
Finnish facts and features, from festival notes to essays about churches and religion in Finland.

FRANCE

All of France

Maison de la France

www.franceguide.com
All of France, all the travel tips, all the festivals. Strangely, for the official site of a country lauded for its cuisine, the section on food and restaurants offers a sparse selection. Good regional coverage, although one or two pages are still under construction.

Tourism in France

www.tourisme.fr/us/index.htm
Complete with a section entitled 'A selection of unwonted stays to discover France', this is a slightly strange but extremely useful site with maps and a good list of links to all things French, and the ability to search under regions or interests - the latter covers everything from casinos to gastronomy.

French Airports

www.aeroport.fr
Select from 29 airports from the drop-down list or by clicking on a region and get all the related information.

France: local sites

For further information on specific regions, try the following sites:

Aix-en-Provence

www.aixenprovencetourism.com

Bordeaux

www.bordeaux-tourisme.com

Brittany

www.brittanytourism.com

Burgundy

www.burgundy-tourism.com

Champagne-Ardennes

www.tourisme-champagne-ard.com

Corsica

www.corsica.net

Les Deux Alpes

www.2alpeservices.com

Loire Valley

www.loirevalleytourism.com

Lorraine

www.cr-lorraine.fr

Lourdes

www.lourdes-france.com/bonjour.htm

Lyon

www.ec-lyon.fr/tourisme/Lyon

Marseille and environs

www.beyond.fr/villages/marseille.html

Nice/French Riviera

www.nice-coteazur.org

Normandy

www.normandy-tourism.org

Paris

www.paris-touristoffice.com

Provence

www.provence.guideweb.com

Provence-Alpes-Côte d'Azur

www.crt-paca.fr

Rhône-Alpes

www.rhonealpes-tourisme.com

Toulouse

www.mairie-toulouse.fr

Val d'Isere

www.valdisere.com

Versailles

www.mairie-versailles.fr

GABON

Destination Gabon

www.lonelyplanet.com/destinations/africa/gabon/attractions.htm

Good sites on Gabon are scarce – Lonely Planet's information fills the gap.

THE GAMBIA

The Gambia National Tourist Office

www.thegambia-touristoff.co.uk

Although this site hasn't been updated for some time, there are plenty of useful details for travellers to Gambia under 'General Information'.

The Republic of The Gambia's Web Page

www.gambia.com

Summarised historical and geographical information, and very basic details in the tourism section on visa requirements and internal transport.

GEORGIA

Virtual Georgia

www.opentext.org.ge/
Click on 'About Georgia' for a long list of facts on everything from geography to religion in this former Soviet state.

GERMANY

Germany Wunderbar

www.germany-tourism.de
Entertaining, detailed site, with plenty of background information, good regional information on each one of the states, and a travel checklist.

Welcome to Munich

www.munich-tourist.de
Aerial views of the city, the low-down on city events, including the Oktoberfest and other tips for travellers.

Bavaria Alpine Net Guide

www.bavaria.com
The culture and travel sections provide background, a selection of links provides more information on this area.

Berlin

www.berlin.de
From the wall to the New Berlin – this site looks at Berlin past and Berlin present, with tips on how to enjoy the latter.

Hamburg Highlights

www.hamburg-highlights.de
A guide to what to do in Hamburg, with details of museums, shops, restaurants, bars and, to get an idea of the setting for it all, virtual views.

Stuttgart Marketing

www.stuttgart-tourist.de
All about Stuttgart, from festivals to exhibitions.

Frankfurt Information

www.frankfurt.de
Not all the information on this site is in English yet, but will be soon. In any case, there is enough information here to get an idea of the city, and as it is the official site, they answer email queries.

Welcome to Leipzig

www.lipsia.de
Basic information on Leipzig, with some pages waiting to be translated into English.

GHANA

An Introduction to Ghana

www.interknowledge.com/Ghana
Background to Ghana and its people, with a look at attractions and adventures.

GREECE

InfoXenios – Greek National Tourist Office

www.hri.org/infoxenios
Nominated as one of the best tourism web sites on Europe, and understandably so. Easy to navigate and full of information on Greece and its islands.

Travel in Greece

www.travel-greece.com
Good general site on Greece, providing regional information, a background to the art and culture and a recipe list.

Athens Survival Guide

www.athensguide.com

One man's personal experience of Athens, translated into an extremely useful and insightful site.

Athens Today

www.athens-today.gr
The official site.

Athens International Airport

www.athensairport-2001.gr
A guide to the gateway to Athens.

Crete TourNet

www.crete.tournet.gr
Digital maps for exploring the island, a guide to speaking basic Greek and a host of facts about the mythology, culture and attractions of Crete.

Welcome to the Ionian Islands

www.ionian-islands.com
The complete travel guide to the Ionian islands of Corfu, Paxoi, Leykada, Ithaki, Cephalonia and Zakynthos.

Rhodes: The City

www.vacation.net.gr/p/cityrhod.html
Background to the ancient city, sightseeing in the old town and some facts about the new town as well.

Kefallonia Links, Stories and Adventures

www.geocities.com/Athens/Agora/6062
A homage to the island now famous as the setting for Captain Corelli's Mandolin.

GREENLAND

Greenland Guide

www.greenland-guide.gl
The official guide, with 1,800 pages about visiting Greenland.

GRENADA

Grenada – Official Travel Guide

www.grenada.org
A comprehensive overview to the Spice Island.

GUATEMALA

Homepage Guatemala

www.guatemala.travel.com.gt
Official site with general information and travel tips.

GUINEA

Republic of Guinea

http://bubl.ac.uk/link/r/republicofguinea.htm
Directory of good links to information about Guinea.

GUINEA-BISSAU

Guinea Bissau Travel Guide

www.newafrica.com/travelguides/guineabissau.asp
Brief but fairly detailed overview from New Africa guides.

GUYANA

Travel Guyana

www.interknowledge.com/guyana
Official site for the place where Caribbean meets South American.

HAITI

Island Connoisseur – The Republic of Haiti

www.caribbeansupersite.com/haiti.index,htm
Travel information, maps, weather, a guide to the beaches, flora, fauna, history and regions of Haiti.

HONDURAS

Honduras.com

www.honduras.com
Latest Honduras news and general information. Click on the 'Travel' section in the left hand list for a detailed breakdown of where to go and what to do in Honduras.

HUNGARY

Hungarian Home Page

www.fsz.bme.hu/hungary/homepage.html
Click on the map or headings below the map for links to further information – some pages are in Hungarian only, but there is plenty of information available in English.

Budapest Week

www.budapestweek.com
What's on in Budapest.

ICELAND

Icelandic Tourist Board

www.icetourist.is
The official site of the land of glaciers, erupting volcanoes and the midnight sun, evocative and useful.

Reykjavik

www.rvk.is
Well-presented site with detailed city information, including where to eat, concerts, daytours from Reykjavik, galleries, hiking areas, shopping, sailing, museums, and much more.

Keflavik International Airport

www.randburg.com/airport/
Passenger facilities at Iceland's main airport, and a selection of useful links.

INDIA

Welcome to India

www.indiatouristoffice.co.uk

The official tourist office site, with rigorous detail. Click on 'Information' for a list of do's and don'ts, health regulations and handy travel tips. Different regions are exlored in 'Destinations' – simply click on the virtual map.

India Travel Times

www.indiatraveltimes.com/

The list on the right gives regional details, the list on the left gives insights into Indian life, for example yoga or Ayurvedic medicine.

All India

www.allindia.com

Takes a look at major Indian tourist centres and eight main cities.

India City

www.indiacity.com

Information on Indian cities from Agra to Varanasi.

Discover India

www.pugmarks.com/d-india

Full of pictures and articles, this is the online version of the magazine 'Discover India', published by the Indian Tourism Development Corporation.

Maps of India

www.mapsofindia.com

Maps galore – from road, air network and railway maps to maps highlighting the best areas for a bungy jump, or cinema halls in Mumbai or Dehli, or the progress of the South West Monsoon.

Templenet – The Comprehensive Indian Temple Website

www.templenet.com

This site pays homage to over 2,000 temples in India, and gives pointers on the different architectural styles, festival traditions and temple etiquette.

Festivals and Fairs of India

www.indiafairs.com/index.html
All the fun of the fairs and festivals in India, from well known celebrations such as Holi and Diwali to Lohri, which marks the last days of winter in the Punjab.

Times of India

www.timesofindia.com
The classic Indian newspaper.

India Express

www.indiaexpress.com
Mainstream Indian news reports.

Indian Railways

www.indianrailway.com
The largest train network in the world, Indian Railways carries more than 11 million passengers in a day. This site is a good starting point if you're planning on joining them, with timetables, tourist information and more.

Raj Tourism

www.rajtourism.com/html/travels_main.html
Jodhpur, Jaipur and other cities and attractions of this colourful and historical state.

Darjeeling

www.visit-darjeeling.com
Travellers' tips on Darjeeling – the hill resort famous for tea and stunning views of the Himalayas.

Welcome to Goa

www.goacom.com
When to go to Goa, and what to do and see in this popular holiday destination.

Bengal on the Net

www.bengalonthenet.com
Lists news, events and attractions in Calcutta and Bengal.

Department of Tourism, Kerala

www.keralatourism.org
Kerala is fast growing in popularity as a destination. This official site outlines the attractions.

Punjab Online

www.punjabonline.com
Land of the five rivers, home to the Golden Temple and one of India's most productive states, the Punjab is explored in some detail by this site.

Gujarat Online

www.gujaratonline.com
General news and information on Gujarat, with current emphasis on the aftermath of the earthquake that devastated this region.

Library Kashmir Virtual

www.clas.ufl.edu/users/gthursby/kashmir/travel.htm
Safe virtual journeys to Kashmir, through a series of links related to this beautiful but troubled region.

Assam.org

www.assam.org
News and articles on this north-eastern state of India, nestled among the Himalayan foothills.

INDONESIA

Tourism Indonesia

www.tourismindonesia.com
This official site covers the main attractions and also has some interesting facts and figures, including the cost of renting a house in Jakarta for a month and average taxi fares from the airport.

Bali Paradise Online

www.bali-paradise.com
History, religion, arts and crafts, as well as practical travel tips.

Guide Book to East Java

www.eastjava.com
Basic information on eastern Java.

Jakarta Online

www.jakarta.go.id
Places of interest and things to do in Jakarta, and some background information on art, history and Indonesian cuisine.

IRAN

Iran Online

www.irannline.com
Click on the 'Iran Hall' section for links to information on everything from economics to food and culture in Iran.

Iran Tourism and Touring Organisation

www.itto.org
A brief round-up of provinces and attractions in Iran.

IRAQ

Arab Net: Iraq

www.arab.net/iraq/iraq_contents.html
Overview of Iraq, with brief summaries on politics, economy, etc.

IRELAND

Irish tourist board

www.ireland.travel.ie
This official site gives comprehensive information on where to go and what to do in Ireland.

Dublin County

www.countydublin.com
A guide to one of the smallest, most interesting counties in Ireland, with plenty of information on Dublin city as well.

Cork City

www.aardvark.ie/cork
Visitor information on the sea port of Cork, Ireland's third city.

Waterford Guide

www.waterford-guide.com
What's on in Waterford, well known for its crystal.

Galway Guide

www.galwayguide.com
A brief look at the attractions of this beautiful Irish destination.

Limerick Life

www.limericklife.com
Limerick has been a popular choice for visitors to Ireland for some time, but has become even more so since it featured as the setting for 'Angela's Ashes', written by Frank McCourt.

ISRAEL

Israel Infotour

www.infotour.co.il
Israel in detail, from the Ministry of Tourism.

Israel

www.goisrael.com
Another official site, this has an interesting section on 'What today's headlines mean to tourists in Israel'.

Israel Airport Authority

www.ben-gurion-airport.com/english/main.htm
Schedules and passenger information on Ben Gurion Airport.

The Jerusalem Website

www.jerusalem.muni.il/english
A look at the stories behind the news, and useful information for travellers, including a section on culture and entertainment.

Eilat Online

www.eilat.net
Bars and beaches explored, and a whole lot more, including the history of the city.

Nazareth City Offical Website

www.nazareth.muni.il
The largest Arab-populated city in Israel, Nazareth is also home to the Basilica of the Annunciation. Many pages are still under construction, but it does provide a basic background to the city.

Tel Aviv City Connection

www.tel-aviv.cc
A whole host of links to information about Tel Aviv.

ITALY

Italian State Tourist Office

www.enit.it
The official site, with a wealth of information. Click on the map for a breakdown of attractions in a particular region.

In Italy Online

www.initaly.com
A labour of love, this site is mantained by a host of Italophiles who have put together an impressive collection of facts, figures and features on the country, including information on the different regions, on books about Italy and films set in Italy.

Italian State Railways

www.fs-on-line.com
Rail and timetable information.

Rome and Italy in Virtual Reality

www.compart-multimedia.com/virtuale/
A virtual guide to Rome, Pisa and Naples.

Rome Guide

www.romeguide.it
Maps, museums, monuments, music and much more.

Roma

www.romaturismo.it
Attractions and current events in the happening Eternal City.

Aeroporti di Roma

www.adr.it
Information on flights and facilities at Fiumicino and Ciampino airports.

A Key to Milan

http://users.iol.it/kiwi.milano/mi_english.htm
Selected pages from a guidebook to Milan, providing basic information on sightseeing and practical tips for visitors, including details of Milan's airports.

Venice City Guide

www.elmoro.com/
Basic information on what to see and do in Venice.

Virtual Venice

www.virtualvenice.com
An interactive map of Venice.

Venice Airport

www.veniceairport.it/vce/ita/home.asp
The ins and outs of Venice's Marco Polo Airport.

Firenze.net

www.english.firenze.net
Art and culture, monuments and museums in Florence.

Your Way to Florence

www.arca.net/florence.htm
Florence for visitors, with opening times and a map.

Uffizi Gallery

www.uffizi.firenze.it/welcomeE.html
Florence is home to an astonishing amount of significant art, and much of it is housed in the Uffizi. This official site has all the useful information on opening hours, as well as a map of the vast gallery.

Bologna

http://archiginnasio.dsnet.it/engl_bologna.html
An eclectic mixture of travelogue and facts about Bologna, by an American living in the city.

Verona

www.tourism.verona.it/index_en.shtml
Art, history and practical travel information for the city immortalised by Shakespeare's 'Romeo and Juliet' .

Parma

www.parmaitaly.com
Parma is famous for its Prosciutto and Parmesan cheese, but the capital of Emilia-Romagna has much more to offer, as this site convincingly demonstrates.

Perugia Online

www.perugiaonline.com
Concise, practical information on this hilltop city.

Assisi Tourist Guide

www.assisionline.net
All the essential information on this popular pilgrimage site, home to art by Giotta, Cimabue and Simone Martini amongst others.

Best of Sicily Travel Guide

www.bestofsicily.com
Detailed information on all things Sicilian.

Capri Web

www.capriweb.com
Photos and notes from the Isle of Capri and the Bay of Naples.

JAMAICA

Jamaica Tourist Board

www.jamaicatravel.com
How to enjoy Jamaica – where to go and what to do – plus a useful list of Jamaican facts, from public holidays to local customs.

Virtual Jamaica

www.virtualjamaica.com
Click on the map for related information and photographs.

JAPAN

Guide to Japan

www.japan-guide.com
General information on aspects of both modern and traditional Japan, with a good section on living in Japan.

Japan Travel Updates

www.jnto.go.jp
Travel tips and planning advice from the Japanese Tourist Organisation, with good regional information and a look at plans for the forthcoming football World Cup.

Ski Japan

www.skijapanguide.com
Japan has over 600 resorts, and this site covers the main ones. It also takes a look at the whole 'Ski-Japan' experience, which includes being within earshot of 'J-pop' or Eighties rock on the slopes and soaking in onsen (natural hot springs) with a steaming sake.

Planet Tokyo

www.pandemic.com/tokyo

Interesting, informative survival guide to Japanese culture, with handy hints on etiquette and a good guide to eating out in Tokyo.

Hiroshima Home Page

www.hiroshima.org
Basic information on Hiroshima. The Beauty Place section is not a list of salons but of beautiful places to see.

Tokyo Meltdown

www.bento.com/tleisure.html
Information about and links to every aspect of life in Tokyo.

Fukuoka Now!

www.fukuoka-now.com
Guide to the Fukuoka prefecture, including an events listing.

Wonderful Osaka

www.geocities.com/Hollywood/Screen/3033
A quick look at Osaka, fondly delivered by a local.

Kyoto City Tourism

http://raku.city.kyoto.jp/sight_apr.html
No-frills site for getting around Kyoto and what to see and do.

JORDAN

Jordan Tourism Board

www.tourism.com.jo
Useful and inspiring site, with evocative descriptions and handy tips on currrency, customs, etiquette, medical care and much more.

KAZAKHSTAN

Welcome to the Official Kazakhstan

www.president.kz/
So official that it is owned by the president, this site delivers quite a formal lesson on the history, culture and attractions of the state.

Kenya

Africa Online - Kenya

www.africaonline.co.ke
Articles, events and links to the main newspapers in Kenya.

Visit Kenya

www.visit-kenya.com
Scroll down the home page for information on specific regions, a slide show, and links to useful information for visitors, which includes details of main airports.

Virtual Nairobi

www.kenyaweb.com/vnairobi/
Comprehensive guide to the city that was once a collection of shacks and tracks but is now a metropolis. Includes where to eat, what to see, transport, communications and a guide to Swahili.

Kiribati

Tourism Council of the South Pacific

www.tcsp.com
Click on the destination section and follow the links for information on Kiribati, or Christmas Island as it is sometimes called.

Korea (Democratic People's Republic)

Democratic People's Republic of Korea

www.kimsoft.com/dprk.htm
Features links covering current issues, military affairs, travel and business and other information about North Korea.

Korea (Republic)

Korea National Tourism Organisation

www.knto.or.kr/english/index.html
Official low-down on where to go and what to see in South Korea.

Seoul City

www.metro.seoul.kr/eng/travel/index.html
Meticulously detailed site, surveying all the attractions that Seoul has to offer. Includes news and events and information on shopping and Korean cuisine.

KUWAIT

Kuwait

www.mideasttravelnet.com/mideastsite/kuwait/cs.htm
Basic but useful overview of Kuwait, including information on red tape and visas.

KYRGYZSTAN

Destination Kyrgyzstan

www.lonelyplanet.com/destinations/central_asia/kyrgyzstan/
Many travellers find this the most welcoming of the Central Asian Republics. These information-packed pages show why.

LAOS

Visit Laos

www.visit-laos.com
This informative site covers when to visit and what to pack, tips on money, health, visas, plus a list of do's and dont's.

LATVIA

Latvia Tourist Board

www.latviatravel.com
This official site outlines the main attractions of this former Soviet state, and provides practical travel tips too.

Riga in Your Pocket

www.inyourpocket.com/Latvia/Riga_home.shtml
Riga by day and Riga by night, in plenty of detail.

LEBANON

Ministry of Tourism

www.lebanon-tourism.gov.lb
Easy to navigate and full of information, this site features a potted country profile and details on events and activities.

LESOTHO

Travel Guide to Africa – Lesotho

www.go2africa.com/lesotho
Well-designed site, covering all the basics for visitors plus some useful local phrases.

LIBERIA

InfoHub Liberia Travel Guide

www.infohub.com/travelguide/traveller/africa/liberia.html
A page of links to information on Liberia, including the US State Department's travel advisory on this troubled country.

LIBYA

LibyaOnline

www.libyaonline.com
Libya is emerging as a new, exciting travel destination. This site covers all the basics in some depth.

LIECHTENSTEIN

Travel Org – Liechtenstein

www.travel.org/liechtens.html
Contains links to the most useful pages on this little-visited European country.

LITHUANIA

Lithuanian State Department of Tourism

www.tourism.lt
General information, links to museums, regional details, forthcoming events and details of the various health resorts.

LUXEMBOURG

Luxembourg National Tourist Office

www.ont.lu
A site so detailed it even lists extracts from the Luxembourg highway code. Plenty of equally useful but more inspiring information is available on these pages.

MACEDONIA

Macedonia FAQ

http://faq.macedonia.org/
The category list on the left reveals a wealth of information on everything from art, cuisine, politics and travel. The travel section has some handy tips under 'What every foreigner should know when travelling to Macedonia'.

MADAGASCAR

Madagascar – The Rainbow Island

www.dstc.edu.au/au/staff/andry/mada.html
The fauna, flora, history, culture of Madagascar, as well as practical information for visitors.

MALAWI

Malawi - The Warm Heart of Africa

www.members.tripod.com/~malawi/
Places to visit, a detailed map, business and travel information

and a guide to learning the national language of Chichewa can all be found on this helpful site.

MALAYSIA

Malaysia Home Page

www.interknowledge.com/malaysia
Where to go, what to see, what to do, and much more on this well-laid-out site.

Virtual Borneo

www.virtual-borneo.com
Information and links for Sarawak and Sabah.

MALDIVES

Visit Maldives

www.visitmaldives.com
There are almost 2000 islands in the Maldives. This site makes it much easier to find the perfect one, and offers information on culture, etiquette, diving and environmental concerns.

MALI

Destination Mali

www.lonelyplanet.com/destinations/africa/mali
Vital statistics and facts for travellers to Mali, including money and costs, when to go and a look at the main attractions.

MALTA

It's Malta

www.visitmalta.com
This site is a little light on visual content, but heavy on text and heavy on information – a comprehensive guide to Malta.

Malta International Airport

www.maltairport.com
Arrivals, departures and passenger facilities.

MARSHALL ISLANDS

Marshall Islands Visitors Authority

www.yokwe-yok.com
Gateway to information and links on the Marshall Islands and their atolls, including Bikini.

MAURITANIA

Destination Mauritania

www.lonelyplanet.com/destinations/africa/mauritania
One of the least visited countries in the world: to see more than sand requires some planning – and this site will help.

MAURITIUS

Mauritius Welcomes You

www.mauritius.net
Mark Twain said: "God created Mauritius and then the heavens." This site gives more practical data – what to see, where to eat, etc.

Airports of Mauritius

http://mauritius-airport.intnet.mu/
A site plan, flight and tourist information and passenger facilities for Sir Seewoosagur Ramgoolam International Airport.

MEXICO

Mexico Government Tourist Office

www.mexico-travel.com
Mexico past and present, with good regional information and a comprehensive list of handy travel tips – which credit cards are most commonly accepted, what to pack and more.

Meet Mexico

www.meetmexico.gob.mx
Created by their UK embassy, this is an entertaining and thorough overview of the country, from national symbols to food and drink.

Mexico Connect

www.mexconnect.com
Online magazine on all things Mexican, with an eclectic and enjoyable collection of articles ranging from 'Buses in Mexico' to 'Never, Ever, Play Poker With a Mexican Jesuit'.

Mexico Online

www.mexonline.com
Directory of links to all things Mexican, from real estate information to local news.

Our Mexico

www.ourmexico.com
Devoted to independent travel in Mexico, with articles, reviews and a directory of businesses and services, plus moderated forums.

Guide to Acapulco

www.acapulco.com
The complete lowdown on going loco.

Welcome to Cancun

www.gocancun.com
The official guide to Cancun, known for its beaches and as the gateway to Mexico's Mundo Maya region – the Mayan world.

San Jose Del Cabo

www.bajaexpo.com/cities/sanjose.htm
Information not just on San Jose Del Cabo but on the whole of the Baja Peninsula.

Puerto Vallarta

www.puertovallarta.net
The official website for the second-most-visited resort in Mexico.

Tijuana Mexico

www.sdro.com/tj.htm
Details on the attractions of this border town, where casinos, handicraft shops and plastic surgery centres vie for attention.

MICRONESIA

Welcome to the Federated States of Micronesia

www.visit-fsm.org
The four states of Chuuk, Yap, Kosrae and Pohnpei and their 607 islands make up the Federated States. This official site looks at the highlights of all four states and offers useful tips for visitors.

MOLDOVA

Destination Moldova

www.lonelyplanet.com/destinations/europe/moldova/
Background and useful travel tips for travellers to this newly formed ex-Soviet republic state.

MONACO

Monaco Guide

www.monaco.mc/monaco/index.html
A look at the history, culture, events and attractions.

Monte-Carlo Online

www.monte-carlo.mc
From casinos to the Grand Prix, from buying real estate to investment, this site covers the main areas of interest in Monte-Carlo.

MONGOLIA

Travel Mongolia

www.travelmongolia.com/
Basic travel information, images of Mongolia and links to further information about the country and its culture.

Morocco

Welcome to Morocco

www.mincom.gov.ma/english/e_page.html
General information on the regions and culture of Morocco, useful for background knowledge.

Adventures of Morocco

http://i-cias.com/morocco/
Probably the most detailed site on Morocco, with good coverage of different regions and cities, as well as a nifty list of basic tips on visas, getting around, currencies, safety and health.

Morocco FAQ

www.morocco-faq.com/
Answers to frequently asked questions about Morocco, which range from 'Where should I go?' to 'Will I catch anything?' and 'Will I be as dry as the desert?'

Morocco Bound

http://tayara.com/club/mrocbd1.htm
As well as links to resources on Morocco, this site reviews related publications, from guide books to the works of Paul Bowles.

Mozambique

Destination Mozambique

www.lonelyplanet.com/destinations/africa/mozambique
Facts for travellers, including visas, health risks, when to go and a useful general introduction to Mozambique.

Myanmar

The Golden Land

www.myanmar.com
The official version, with links to state-owned papers, a nine-volume section entitled 'The Truth' and regional attractions.

Destination Myanmar

www.lonelyplanet.com/dest/sea/myan.htm
The unofficial version, full of facts and information on money, visas, regulations and when and where to go.

NAMIBIA

Namibia Tourism

www.iwwn.com.na/namtour
Evocative descriptions of the different regions and national parks in Namibia, as well as travel tips and news.

NAURU

Nations of the Commonwealth: Nauru

www.tbc.gov.bc.ca/cwgames/country/Nauru/nauru.html
A long address for a small coral atoll, providing a potted profile.

NEPAL

Travellers' Nepal

www.catmando.com/tn/
Things to do and see in the land where Lord Buddha was born.

Welcome Nepal

www.welcomenepal.com
General information on Nepal and its culture from the Nepal Tourist Board.

THE NETHERLANDS

Visit Holland

www.visitholland.com
This official site is easy to navigate and full of facts on everything from the main cities and destinations to art, culture and museums.

Visit Amsterdam

www.visitamsterdam.nl
Amsterdam has 165 canals and 206 paintings by Van Gogh. This site has information on every attraction, details of events and how to get maximum enjoyment there. It also lists what to avoid.

Amsterdam Airport Schiphol

www.schiphol.nl
Flight information and facilities at the main gateway to Holland.

Delft

www.vvvdelft.nl/eng/index.html
The official source on all aspects of this historic city.

NEW ZEALAND

All of New Zealand

New Zealand Travel Planner

www.travelplanner.co.nz
A map of New Zealand which can calculate driving distances, a currency button which translates money into New Zealand dollars, information on visas, customs allowances, health, and a good selection of related travel articles – this site is useful and inspiring.

Pure New Zealand

www.purenz.com
This official tourist board site is crammed with detail on all things Kiwi, plus short travelogues from enthusiastic visitors.

North Island

Auckland

www.aucklandnz.com

Bay of Plenty

www.visitplenty.co.nz *and* www.nztauranga.com

Christchurch and Canterbury

www.christchurchnz.net

The Coromandel

www.centralnorthnz.co.nz

Eastland/Gisborne

www.gisbornenz.com

Great Barrier

www.greatbarrier.co.nz *and* www.great-barrier.com

Hawkes Bay

www.hawkesbaynz.co.nz

Northland/Bay of Islands

www.northland.org.nz *and* www.twincoast.co.nz

Rotorua

www.rotouanz.com

Taupo

www.laketauponz.com

Waikato

www.waikatonz.co.nz

Wairarapa

www.wairarapanz.com

Wanganui

www.wanganui.com

Wellington

www.wellingtonnz.com

South Island

Auckland International Airport

www.auckland-airport.co.nz
Passenger information and airport maps, as well as services and shopping at Auckland Airport.

Dunedin/Coastal Otago

www.cityofdunedin.com

Fiordland

www.fiordland.org.nz

Marlborough

www.destinationmarlborough.com

Mount Cook/Mackenzie Country

www.mtcook.org.nz

Nelson

www.nelsonnz.com

Otago

www.tco.org.nz

Queenstown

www.queenstown-nz.co.nz

Southland

www.southland.org.nz

Wanaka

www.wanaka.co.nz

West Coast

www.west-coast.co.nz

NICARAGUA

Nicaraguan Insititute of Tourism

www.intur.gob.ni
Answers frequently asked questions about travel to Nicaragua, and showcases the main attractions in pictures, maps and words.

NIGER

Destination Niger

www.lonelyplanet.com/destinations/africa/niger/
Detailed information on the main attractions, and plenty of practical tips for travellers.

NIGERIA

Motherland Nigeria

www.motherlandnigeria.com
Comprehensive collection of links and information about all things Nigerian, including the people, the holidays and festivals, the music, the food and sport, as well as a travel specific section.

NIUE

Niue Tourism Office

www.niueisland.com
A wealth of information on this South Seas island, with a look at local festivals and traditions, including the haircutting and ear piercing ceremonies.

NORWAY

Visit Norway

www.visitnorway.com/en/
An A-Z of travel facts, frequently asked questions, main attractions, weather reports and some stunning shots.

Norwegian Scenery

www.norwegian-scenery.com
More words than pictures, this site covers Norwegian culture and science, economy, food, geography, government, history and nature and the great outdoors in great detail.

Clickwalk Norway

www.clickwalk.no/indexe.html
Virtual walks in Norwegian cities via photography and maps.

Online Guide to Oslo

www.osloguide.net/
A slightly fiddly interactive map to Oslo, providing details of museums, restaurants and shops, and links to further information about Oslo and Norway.

OMAN

The Sultanate of Oman

www.mocioman.org
The tourism section of this site from the Minsitry of Commerce and Industry is easy to navigate and provides a quick overview of the Sultanate.

PALAU

Palau – Adventure in Paradise

www.visit-palau.com
Palau is a 400-mile-long archipelago surrounded by rich marine life. This site covers all its attractions and provides tips for visitors.

PAKISTAN

Welcome to Pakistan

www.tourism.gov.pk
The official site, with regional information, and basic notes on everything from history to entertainment.

The Official Pakistan Page

www.pak.org
Links to Pakistani news, features, books, sport, businesses, politics, fashion, music, poetry and more.

Adil Najan's Pakistan

www.mit.edu/people/anajam/pakistan.html
A personal view of Pakistan, with an unofficial guided tour and links to related sites.

Islamabad

www.islamabad.net/
A look at Pakistan's capital city, with links to offical Pakistani sites and a section on Islam.

Welcome to Lahore

www.alephx.com/lahore
Once the capital of the Mughul ruler Akbar, and now Pakistan's second-largest city, Lahore is explored in some detail on this site.

Karachi

www.alephx.org/karachi
City guide to Karachi, from bazaars to restaurants, with listings of where to go and what to do.

Quetta

www.alephx.com/quetta
Strategically located where the boundaries of Iran and Afghanistan meet Pakistan, Quetta is the stronghold of the western frontier. Its other charms are described on this site.

Peshawar

www.rpi.edu/dept/union/paksa/www/html/pakistan/
peshawar.html
The geography and provinces of 'The place at the frontier' – Peshawar, given its name by Mughal emperor Akbar.

PANAMA

Panama Info

www.panamainfo.com
Visitor information, frequently asked questions and attractions in Panama, from beaches to mountians.

PAPUA NEW GUINEA

Papua New Guinea – Tourism Promotion Authority

www.paradiselive.org.pg
An official break-down of the adventures and attractions available in Papau New Guinea.

PARAGUAY

Destination Paraguay

www.lonelyplanet.com/destinations/south_america/paraguay/
PJ O'Rourke once wrote: 'Paraguay is nowhere and famous for nothing', then fell in love with the place on a working visit. This Lonely Planet site explores the country's charms and dispenses the usual sound advice for travellers.

PERU

Virtual Peru

www.virtualperu.net
Brief, to-the-point information about the people, regions, the culture and history of Peru.

An Introduction to Lima

www.interknowledge.com/peru/lima/
An informative look at Lima, Peru's cultural and business centre. This site also contains details and travel tips on Peru in general.

PHILIPPINES

Philippines

www.filipino.com
Basic information on the main islands and tips on currency, customs regulations, what to wear, tipping and weather.

Leg Manila

http://cityguide.legmanila.com/
A what's on guide for the capital of the Philippines.

POLAND

Polish National Tourist Office

www.polandtour.org
General information about Poland, travel notes, a look at the different regions and cities and their culture and art.

Magical Kracow

www.krakow.pl
Guide to Krakow, with a map and information on culture and art in the city.

Poland in Sound, Noise and Pictures

www.outdoor.se/artiklar/poland
The creator of this curious site went to Poland equipped with a minidisc recorder, determined to record odd Polish sounds.... The result is a quirky collection of pictures and the corresponding music and noise. One for enthusiasts.

PORTUGAL

Welcome to Portugal

www.portugal.org
Vibrant and detailed site, with an interactive map in the 'Travel and Tourism' section full of information on the different regions.

Algarve Life

www.algarve-life.com
This site offers a potted history of Algarve and more – stories from a local journalist, a video gallery, a list of great things to do which includes the heading 'Eating Sardines' and some practical tips for visitors.

Lisbon pages

www.eunet.pt/lisboa
A town plan, looking at five different areas of Lisbon in some detail, museums, restaurants, bars, fado houses, and practical tips all feature on this user-friendly site.

The Azores Islands Web Pages

www.geocities.com/thetropics/2140/azores.html
Click on the map for incredibly detailed information on each island in the Azores.

Madeira

www.madeiratourism.org
George Bernard Shaw and Winston Churchill both fell under the spell of these islands – this site shows why.

PUERTO RICO

Puerto Rico Tourism

www.prtourism.com
A detailed map, basic information for visitors including what to pack, weather facts and descriptions of the main attractions.

QATAR

Qatar-Info

www.qatar-info.com
General background information on Qatar, practical advice on living or visiting the country, including a section on 'How to Behave'; and details on what to do and see in Qatar.

ROMANIA

Tourism in Romania

www.romtourprom.ro
Useful background information on Romania, its Black Sea resorts, the Danube Delta and Transylvania.

Bucharest Online

www.bucharest.com/bol/
This site offers some general information on the Romanian capital, as well as a potted history and a pictorial city tour.

RUSSIA

Guide to Russia

www.themoscowtimes.com/travel/
An extensive and entertaining reference source from the 'Moscow Times', with practical information on getting around, Russian holidays, contact numbers for embassies and other essentials; as well as articles on the attractions and destinations within this vast country.

Russia Tourism Pages

www.russia-tourism.com
An online directory with links to all things Russian, from restaurants and newspapers to sites on entertainment, language and visas.

Russian Life

www.rispubs.com
Online magazine with assorted articles on daily life, events and arts in Russia.

Museums of Russia

www.museum.ru/defengl.htm
Cultural news and a comprehensive list of official and unofficial museums in Russia, with links to several, including the Hermitage.

A Journey to Moscow

www.moscowcity.com
An easy-to-navigate site, covering points of interest in Moscow from the Kremlin to Old Moscow, and a list of useful facts, including safety advice. The transportation section includes tips on taxis/hiring drivers in Moscow (car rental is generally not recommended, because of 'local traffic peculiarities').

Moscow Life

http://solar.rtd.utk.edu/(tilde)asebrant/life/ml.html
or
www.friends-partners.org/oldfriends/asebrant/life/ml.html
Wonderfully idiosyncratic stories about life in Moscow, written between 1995 and 2001 by local resident Andrey.

Welcome to Moscow

http://all-moscow.ru/index.en.html
Information and links to useful services in Moscow from buying works of art to ordering pizza online. Includes a link to a map of the metro system.

Sheremetyevo International Airport

www.sheremetyevo-airport.ru
This is the main point of entry into Moscow, and this site is useful not just for information on schedules but for the notes on customs, getting into Moscow and general advice for visitors.

The Fresh Guide to St Petersburg

www.online.ru/sp/fresh
Everything for visitors to St Petersburg, including practical advice, travel tips and interesting background information on 'The Venice of the North'.

Lake Baikal Home Page

www.baikal.ru
The deepest lake in the world, and the eighth largest, Lake Baikal is a draw for Russians and tourist alike. This site offers a mixture of eulogies and scientific data.

Chechen Republic Online

www.amina.com
Background to Chechnya, its history and its people, with links to related articles and news, including details of the war with Russia.

Tatarstan on the Internet

www.kcn.ru/tat_en
The history and culture of the Republic of Tatarstan, and a look at its capital, Kazan.

Tourist Sites of Karelia

www.gov.karelia.ru/gov/info/tourism_e.html
Basic information on the main attractions in the picturesque Republic of Kariela, a region of quiet lakes and endless pine forests.

The Unofficial Evenki Home Page

www.spri.cam.ac.uk/people/jeoh2/2evenki.htm
A site dedicated to the Evenki – the indigenous people of Siberia. Traditionally nomadic hunters and herders, their way of life is now under threat as mineral, oil and coal extraction continues to expand across the country.

JSC Tolmachevo Airport

www.tolmachevo.ru
In Novosibirsk, Siberia. Flying via this airport offers a convenient and very cost-effective route from Europe to South-East Asia

RWANDA

Destination Rwanda

www.lonelyplanet.com/destinations/africa/rwanda
Just opening up again as a destination for travellers after the terrible civil war, Rwanda still has many beautiful attractions, particularly amazing mountain views and mountain gorillas. This site has information on all the sights, and practical travel advice too.

St Kitts & Nevis

St Kitts Tourism Authority

www.stkitts-nevis.com
For centuries this volcanic island occupied a critical position in the European struggle for the West Indies. Now it's a popular tourist destination, and this site provides basic information for visitors.

St Lucia

Official Guide to St Lucia

www.st-lucia.com
One of the Windward Islands of the Lesser Antilles, lush St Lucia is a popular destination. This official site describes the attractions and offers travel tips.

St Vincent & the Grenadines

St Vincent & the Grenadines

www.svgtourism.com
Travel and general information, an events calendar and details on the activities and attractions offered by these Caribbean islands.

Samoa

Visit Samoa

www.samoa.co.nz
The official site has general and practical advice for visitors to these Polynesian islands, and a calendar of main events.

San Marino

San Marino

www.sanmarinosite.com
Concise information on this compact republic.

SAO TOME E PRINCIPE

Welcome to São Tomé e Principe

www.saotome.st/
The official site for these islands off the coast of central Africa. Some pages are still under construction but it provides a point of contact for further information.

SAUDI ARABIA

Saudi Arabian Information Centre

www.saudinf.com
A lengthy table of contents covers the historical and cultural background of the country, Islam, oil, and the judicial stystem; while an interactive map gives regional information.

Country Profile Saudi Arabia

www.awo.net/country/overview/crsau.asp
Useful facts and figures, plus a couple of articles relating to travel and entertainment.

SENEGAL

Senegal Online

www.senegal-online.com
The towns, the national parks, the lakes and rivers, the culture – all the attractions Senegal has to offer are outlined here.

SEYCHELLES

Seychelles Tourist Office

www.seychelles.uk.com
Particularly good on the history, culture, peoples, nature and food, this site also has practical tips for travellers to the Seychelles.

SIERRA LEONE

Sierra Leone Web

www.sierra-leone.org
Comprehensive all-in-one resource, with links to information on everything from travel advice and alerts to diamonds and history.

SINGAPORE

New Asia – Singapore

www.travel.com.sg
The drop-down menu offers detailed information on several subjects from attractions to travellers' essentials for the 'Geneva of the East'.

Singapore Infomap

www.sg/
An excellent and extensive range of links to information about Singapore, including art and entertainment, health, food, news and media, government, and general reference.

Unorthodox Singapore

www.geocities.com/thetropics/7222/main.html
Advice on visiting Singapore, written by a resident.

Singapore Changi Airport

www.changi.airport.com.sg
This airport has been voted the best in several categories. This site looks at the facilities, flight information and how to reach the airport. Also customs and health regulations.

SLOVAK REPUBLIC

Slovakia.Org

www.slovakia.org/
Current events, culture, regional information, useful facts for travellers and a good FAQ section which provides a potted history.

Slovak Tourist Board

www.sacr.sk
*This official site is a bit patchy, but does provide basic background
to the country.*

Bratislava

www.eunet.sk/slovakia/bratislava.html
A map, a picture tour and a potted history of the city.

SLOVENIA

Slovenia Tourism Pages

www.slovenia-tourism.com
*Directory of links, with several useful contacts for embassies and
general information about the country.*

Welcome to Slovenia

www.slovenia-tourism.si
*This site is laced with flowery motifs – and language – but delivers
basic information for travellers and takes a look at the main tourist
regions.*

SOLOMON ISLANDS

Solomon Islands Visitors Bureau

www.commerce.gov.sb/Tourism/indexc.htm
*A mixture of information and links, with an interactive map
which provides a more detailed map, a photo gallery and information for specific regions.*

SOMALIA

Somali Website

www.somaliwebsite.com/
Links to current events and useful information on the country.

Infohub Somalia Travel Guide

www.infohub.com/TravelGuide/traveller/africa/somalia.html
Links to travel related information on Somalia.

SOUTH AFRICA

South African Tourism

www.satour.co.uk
An A-Z of fast facts, this site provides practical travel tips, a special interest section including details of game reserves and wine routes, plus suggested itineraries and maps. Comprehensive and user-friendly.

South Africa

www.southafrica.com
An extensive directory of links to all aspects of life in South Africa, with a section devoted to travel information.

South African National Parks

www.parks-sa.co.za
Detailed information on game reserves and national parks in South Africa. As well as lists of animals commonly seen in each park and gate opening times, the site gives emergency numbers and hints on what to pack.

Daily Mail & Guardian

www.mg.co.za
As well as offering news and events, this newspaper site has a section dedicated to travel, with assorted articles on game reserves, art and culture and conservation.

Airports Company South Africa

www.airports.co.za
Passenger information and flight schedules for the main airports.

Garden Route Guide

www.gardenroute.co.za

Follows the popular garden route between Cape Town and Port Elizabeth, and takes a look at other regions as well.

Cape Town and Cape Metropolitan Region

www.gocapetown.co.za
Official site, with details of all the fun to be had in the area, a map and transport information, and A-Z travel tips.

Welcome to Destination Pretoria

www.visitpretoria.co.za
An introduction to the capital of South Africa, with practical information on medical services, transport and trading hours, and an entertainment guide.

KwaZulu Natal

www.tourism-kzn.org
A look at the attractions of this region, including the Dolphin Coast, Drakensburg, Zululand and a profile of Durban.

Time Out Guide to Johannesburg

www.timeout.com/johannesburg
What's on, main sights, travel tips and a guide to eating, drinking and shopping in the city.

Eshayamoya Country

www.eshayamoya.org.za
Kwazulu-Natal, Southern Drakensberg, Pietermarizburg and East Griqualand explored in some depth.

Homesick South Africans

www.arrowweb.com/aris/rsa
Eclectic collection of South African links, some quirky (South African Jokes), some serious (all the local papers).

Artzone

www.artzone.co.za
Art galleries, theatres and cultural events in South Africa.

Powerzone

www.powerzone.co.za
A guide to gigs around South Africa.

South African Wine

www.wine.co.za
South Africa has a reputation for notable wine, and this site looks at the regions dedicated to producing it.

SPAIN

National Tourist Office of Spain

www.tourspain.es
The official website for the third most visited country in the world, with all the essential information on regions, beaches, museums and much more.

All About Spain

www.red2000.com/spain
A regional and city guide, a photo-tour, and a section on 'Country and Culture', full of facts about bullfights, flamenco, famous and infamous fiestas, regional cooking and nightlife.

Bilbao

www.bilbao.net
Culture, events and travel tips for the city of Bilbao.

Andalucia

www.andalucia.org
Andalucia explored, from the volcanic landscapes of the Tabernas Desert to the white peaks of the Sierra Nevada, with a look at historic cities such as Seville and Granada.

Valencia: A Virtual Trip

www.upv.es/cv/valbegin.html
Museums, monuments, culture, gardens, transport, and a look at local traditions in Valencia, backed up by great pictures.

Softguide Madrid

www.softdoc.es
There's enough information on this site to keep both culture vu-lures and hedonists happy, with details on nightlife and museums, galleries and shopping and much more on Madrid.

Barcelona Travel Guide

www.spain.areatravel.net/barcelona
What to do and see in Spain's second largest city.

Catalonia Tourist Guide

www.publintur.es
Choose a city or region from the drop-down menus for background and practical information.

Benidorm Web Guide

www.athenea.com/benidorm
Beaches and bars, churches and city information, safety tips and weather forecasts for this popular Costa Blanca destination.

Balearic Islands

www.red2000.com/spain/baleares/
All the facts about the islands of Mallorca, Menorca, Ibiza, For-mentera and Cabrera.

Canary Islands

www.spaintour.com/canarias.htm
Places of interest and travel tips for Gran Canaria, Lanzarote, Fuerteventura, Tenerife, La Gomera, La Palma and and Hierro.

SRI LANKA

Ceylon Tourist Board

www.lanka.net/ctb
Straightforward site with concise information on the places of in-terest, from Colombo to the Hill Country, beaches to national parks, and tips on travel, culture and religion in Sri Lanka.

SUDAN

Al Sudan

www.sudan.net
A mixture of data and links, this site provides fast facts, plenty of information on Sudanese society and culture, a photo gallery, links to embassies and information on the main cities and attractions.

SURINAM

Surinam Info Desk

www.surinfo.org/
A good introduction to this South American country, with plenty of advice on culture, attitudes and etiquette, practical travel information, and a look at the main attractions which include the largest protected tropical forest area in the world. It is possible to download a visa application form.

SWAZILAND

Tourism in Swaziland

www.swazi.com/tourism
Links to Swazi travel information and tourist attractions.

The Official Swaziland Tourism Site

www.mintour.gov.sz/
The best information on this comprehensive site can be found in 'The Royal Experience' section, which covers the history, culture and main attractions of the country.

SWEDEN

Visitsweden.com

www.visit-sweden.com
The official website, with comprehensive regional and general information for travellers.

Welcome to Stockholm

www.stockholm.se/english

All the necessary information on visiting Stockholm, including an events guide, details on transportation, nightlife, restaurants and more.

CityGuide Sweden

www.cityguide.se

Useful data on dozens of Swedish cities.

LFV

www.lfv.se

Information on all major Swedish airports, including maps of the airports and flight schedules.

SWITZERLAND

My Switzerland

www.switzerlandtourism.ch

This official site is a little fiddly to use but covers the main points for visitors.

Geneva Guide

www.geneva-guide.ch

The alternative guide to Geneva, with an excellent range of facts on what to do in and around the city.

Geneva International Airport

www.gva.ch/en/default.htm

All the necessary data on getting in and out of Geneva.

Zurich Tourism

www.zurichtourism.ch

Easy-to-navigate site, offering details on sights, museums, restaurants and culture in Zurich, complete with a virtual tour of the city.

Basel Tourism

www.baseltourismus.ch
Basel is more than the centre of the pharmaceutical industry, with plenty of attractions and music and jazz festivals. This site has all the details on getting around and having a good time.

Gstaad Online

www.gstaad.ch
What to do and see in Gstaad, summer and winter.

Welcome to Bern

www.berntourismus.ch
Reams of information on Bern, seat of the Swiss government and a UNESCO World Heritage Site.

SYRIA

Ministry of Tourism

www.syriatourism.org
The official site gives detailed information on Syrian culture, destinations and a list of essential facts for travellers.

TAIWAN

Taiwan Tourism Bureau

www.tbroc.gov.tw/
Clicking on the map finds information on the regions, and there is a fair amount of more general detail on attractions and travel tips.

Travel in Taiwan

www.sinica.edu.tw/tit/
Magazine articles on arts, festivals, food, museums and shopping.

TAJIKISTAN

Tajikistan Country Guide

www.tajikstan.com/

A potted profile of Tajikistan, notes on history and culture and a good selection of links to related sites.

TANZANIA

Tanzania Tourist Board

www.tanzania-web.com
This site gives a good overview of the country and is easy to navigate – an interactive map provides details of game parks and reserves and all the other attractions in the land of Kilimanjaro.

Zanzibar Travel Network

www.zanzibar.net
The Spice Island explored in some detail, from ancient Stone Town to the plantations, Jozani Forest and beaches.

THAILAND

Tourism Authority of Thailand

www.tat.or.th
Things to see and do in Thailand, with a look at provinces, attractions, food, festivals and advice for travellers.

Thailand: The Big Picture

www.nectec.or.th/thailand/index.html
Links to information about Thailand, including local papers, and sites about cuisine and learning the language.

Bangkok Thailand Today

www.bangkok.thailandtoday.com
Comprehensive guide to Bangkok and its varied attractions.

TOGO

Republique Togolais

www.republicoftogo.com
News, current events, places of interest and handy travel hints.

TONGA

Tonga Visitors' Bureau

www.vacations.tvb.gov.to
Fast facts, travel tips, sights, activities, history and culture.

Tonga Online

www.tongaonline.com
A mixture of background information and links to other sites on Tonga.

TRINIDAD & TOBAGO

Welcome to Trinidad & Tobago

www.visittnt.com
Information on carnivals, festivals, beaches, eating out and generally having a good time in this popular Caribbean destination.

TUNISIA

The Travel and Tourism Guide to Tunisia

www.tourismtunisia.com
Tunisia from top to toe.

TURKEY

Ministry of Tourism

www.turkey.org/turkey
A country profile, events, culture, and travel information for Turkey, and a selection of links.

Turkish Press

www.turkishpress.com
Daily news and views from Turkey.

Istanbul City Guide

www.istanbulcityguide.com

A complete guide to the city divided into two continents by the Bosphorus.

TURKMENISTAN

Destination Turkmenistan

www.lonelyplanet.com/destinations/central_asia/turk-menistan/
There are very few detailed sites on Turkmenistan – this is probably the best for travellers, and has links to the best of the rest. Also includes information on culture, attractions and events, even though 'Turkmenistan isn't known for its jolly street parades.'

TUVALU

Tuvalu Online

http://members.nbci.com/tuvaluonline/index.htm
Information and links and a look at the history and legends associated with this South Pacific island.

UGANDA

Tourism in Uganda

www.visituganda.com
Quick facts on everything from arrivals and courtesies to road rules, an excellent brief history, and a look at the attractions, parks and reserves, including Bwindi Impenetrable National Park, one of the last homes of the Mountain Gorilla.

UKRAINE

Gateway Ukraine

www.brama.com
Links to information about Ukraine, including traditions and folklore – for instance, the informative and entertaining 'Wedding FAQ'.

Welcome to Ukraine

www.ukraine.org
Basic travel facts and assorted links on Ukraine.

Kyiv Navigator

www.kiev.ua:8101
A photo gallery and addresses and phone numbers for local restaurants, theatres, banks and medical services.

UNITED ARAB EMIRATES

Welcome to the United Arab Emirates

www.uae.org.ae
Five-in-one site, featuring detailed general, social, tourist, business and web guides to the UAE.

Emirates

www.emirates.org
Articles and links about tourism and traditions in the UAE.

Discover Dubai

www.dubaitourism.com
The city often known as the Shopper's Paradise has other attractions on offer, and this site looks at the best.

Go Dubai

www.godubai.com
Magazine-style content covering all aspects of life in Dubai and a section for visitors outlining attractions and advice.

Sharjah International Airport

www.shj-airport.gov.ae
Airport facts and plenty of information about the city of Sharjah, close to Dubai.

UNITED KINGDOM

All of the UK

British Tourist Authority

www.visitbritain.com
Official, efficient and clearly laid out, with comprehensive regional information, details of attractions, activities and events, images of Britain and a good selection of links.

Britannia

www.britannia.com
Published online by Americans, for Americans planning to visit the United Kingdom. But useful for anyone interested in British history, culture and life. Includes virtual tours of Scotland and Wales.

Sightseeing UK

www.sightseeing.co.uk
Culture, history, art and entertainment venues across the UK – covers everything from castles to football grounds.

National Trust

www.nationaltrust.org.uk
Stately homes, fine gardens and natural beautyspots in England, Wales and Northern Ireland (see 'Scotland' for Scottish site).

24 Hour Museum

www.24hourmuseum.org.uk
Simply click on the map for details of and links to museums all around the UK.

BAA Airports

www.baa.co.uk
Travel services and facilities at main UK airports.

Railtrack

www.railtrack.co.uk

The site is slicker and smoother than the actual rail service, with an interactive timetable showing the quickest route between stations. Also includes information and maps for individual stations.

Good Beach Guide

www.goodbeachguide.co.uk
Marine Conservation Society guide to the best of British beaches.

UKonline

www.ukonline.gov.uk
Links to district councils around the UK, providing information about individual communities and things to do and see in local areas.

United Kingdom Travel and Tourist Information

www.travel-library.com/europe/uk
Links to general information and travelogues about the UK.

Knowhere guide

www.knowhere.co.uk
A look at the UK through the eyes of local residents, this is an unedited, rough-and-ready site, offering a mixed bag of personal opinions on British regions and cities.

Freetodo

www.Freetodo.freeserve.co.uk
Guide to free things to do in the UK, from galleries to gardens.

UK Entertainment

www.ukentertainmentguide.co.uk
Details for cinema and film, music and concerts, theatres and musicals, bars and nightclubs around the UK.

Enjoy Britain

www.enjoybritain.co.uk
The famous British countryside, eating out, music venues, attractions and much more explored, plus a selection of links to related websites.

Public Transport Information

www.pti.org.uk/
Comprehensive guide to public transport in Britain, including timetables and passenger facilities.

The Countryside Agency

www.countryside.gov.uk
Information and advice for visitors to the English countryside, including maps linking to regional and local information.

British Waterways

www.britishwaterways.co.uk
The hidden world of Britain's inland waterways revealed, with the help of interactive maps of canals and navigable rivers.

The Ramblers Association

www.ramblers.org.uk
News and advice on countryside and urban walks around the UK.

Classic Pub Walks

www.classicpubwalks.com
Routes linking the country's oldest and most interesting pubs.

London

London Town

www.londontown.com
All the attractions London has to offer are accessible through this official site. Culture, shopping, eating out, clubs, galleries are all covered and the links are extremely useful.

Kids Link London

www.londontown.com/kids
The lowdown on London from children living in the capital.

This is London

www.thisislondon.com

*London news and views, lifestyle and leisure and tourist informa-
tion, all covered in depth on this lively site from the owners of the
local 'Evening Standard' newspaper.*

Time Out

www.timeout.com
*The Londoner's guide to London is also one of the best guides for
visitors to the capital, with information on what's on, what to see
and where to shop, eat and party.*

Transport for London

www.londontransport.co.uk
*Help and advice on travelling around London by tube, bus, and
river services.*

England

BBC Online – England

www.bbc.co.uk/england/
*More than local news around the country – there's live webcams
and information on sport, weather and entertainment too.*

English Heritage

www.english-heritage.org.uk
*Information on protected historic buildings, landscapes and ar-
chaeological sites in England.*

English Tourist Boards

Cumbria Tourist Board

www.golakes.co.uk

East of England Tourist Board

www.eastofenglandtouristboard.com

Heart of England Tourist Board

www.visitheartofengland.com

Northumbria Tourist Board

www.ntb.org.uk

North West Tourist Board

www.visitnorthwest.com

South East England Tourist Board

www.southeastengland.uk.com

Southern Tourist Board

www.gosouth.co.uk

South West Tourism

www.westcountryholidays.com

Yorkshire Tourist Board

www.ytb.org.uk

Scotland

Visit Scotland

www.visitscotland.org
Official and comprehensive, this site looks at the main attractions to be found in beautiful Scotland, and has good links, practical advice and a FAQ section.

Walk Scotland

www.walkscotland.com
Several suggestions for taking a walk in Scotland, with a new one added every week, practical information for climbers and hikers, a look at gear, assorted links and jokes.

National Trust for Scotland

www.nts.org.uk
A guide to the places of historic interest or natural beauty safeguarded by the National Trust.

Historic Scotland

www.historic-scotland.gov.uk
From Edinburgh Castle to Glasgow Cathedral to Linlithgow Palace, this site has details on all the major historical sites in Scotland.

The Mountaineering Council of Scotland

www.mountaineering-scotland.org.uk/
News and features, as well as advice on enjoying Scotland's mountains.

Scottish regions

Aberdeen & Grampian Tourist Board

www.agtb.org

Angus & Dundee Tourist Board

www.angusanddundee.co.uk

Argyll, the Isles, Loch Lomond, Stirling & Trossachs Tourist Board

www.scottish.heartlands.org/

Ayrshire & Arran Tourist Board

www.ayrshire-arran.com

Dumfries & Galloway Tourist Board

www.galloway.co.uk

Edinburgh and Lothians Tourist Board

www.edinburgh.org

Edinburgh First City

www.firstcity.force9.co.uk

Glasgow Virtual City Guide

www.virtualglasgow.com

Greater Glasgow & Clyde Valley Tourist Board

www.seeglasgow.com

Highlands of Scotland Tourist Board

www.host.co.uk

Orkney's Official Website

www.orkney.com

Perthshire Tourist Board

www.perthshire.co.uk

Shetlands Island Tourism

www.shetland-tourism.co.uk

The Western Isles Tourist Board

www.witb.co.uk

Wales

Welsh Tourist Board

www.visitwales.com
News, events and information on all the attractions in Wales.

Welcome to Wales

www.croeso.com
Regional information from Aberdovey to Wrexham, and related links.

North Wales Tourism

www.nwt.co.uk
The borderlands, the Isle of Anglesey, Snowdonia and local coastal resorts explored.

CADW: Welsh Historic Monuments

www.cadw.wales.gov.uk
Cadw is a Welsh word which means 'to keep', and the organisation

conserves historic sites in Wales. This site has details for all of them.

Pembrokeshire Online

www.pembrokeshire-online.co.uk/index.htm
Details about one of the most popular destinations in Wales.

Tour Cardiff

www.tigerbay.com/newcity
All the essential information on Cardiff, easily accessed through an A-Z index or through a map of the city centre.

Virtual Portmerion

www.virtualportmeirion.com
Portmerion rose in popularity after being the setting for the TV series 'The Prisoner', but is an attractive destination in its own right.

City of Swansea

www.swansea-gower.demon.co.uk
The lowdown on Swansea, with additional information on Mumbles and Gower.

Llanfair PG

http://llanfairpwllgwyngyllgogerychwyrndrobwllllantysilio-
gogogoch.co.uk
The longest place name (and URL) in Britain belongs to this town.

Northern Ireland

Northern Ireland Tourist Board

www.ni-tourism.com
Although compact in size, Northern Ireland has a large variety of sights and attractions. This site looks at all of them.

Northern Irish regions

Belfast City

www.tourism.belfastcity.gov.uk/index.html

Armagh: Travel and Visitor Guide

www.armagh-visit.com

Down District Council

www.downdc.gov.uk

Local Ireland: Local Antrim

www.antrim.local.ie

Welcome to County Fermanagh

www.countyfermanagh.com

Welcome to County Tyrone

www.countytyrone.com

Isle of Man

Welcome to the Isle of Man

www.isle-of-man.com
Manx information, news, events and links.

Channel Islands

States of Guernsey Tourist Board

www.guernseytouristboard.com
Guernsey through the seasons, and a guide to what to do and which beaches to visit.

Jersey Web

www.jersey.co.uk
This collection of links is a one-stop shop for information about Jersey.

UNITED STATES OF AMERICA

All of the USA

USA Tourism

www.usatourism.com
Straightforward site with links to information on each state.

AreaGuides USA

www.areaguides.net
Click on the state of your choice for a directory of links on everything from local restaurants to medical services.

Desert USA

www.desertusa.com
From Stinkbugs to Tumbleweed, this site looks at all the deserts.

US National Parks

www.us-national-parks.net/
Details of all the national parks in the US, from Acadia to Zion.

Ski Guide

www.ski-guide.com
A guide to all the skiing and snowboarding resorts in the US and Canada.

Rocky Mountain International

www.rmi-realamerica.com
A guide to the American Rockies, which extend through Wyoming, South Dakota, Montana and Idaho.

States in the USA

Alabama

Unforgettable Alabama

www.touralabama.org

Alaska

Travel Alaska

www.travelalaska.com

Alaska Tourism and Travel Guide

www.alaskanet.com/Tourism

North to Alaska

www.north-to-alaska.com
A look at the famous Alaska Highway, which covers an awesome 2647km (or 1645miles), from Fairbanks to Dawson Creek, British Columbia.

Department of Transportation

www.dot.state.ak.us/external/tmphome.html
Information on Alaska's Marine Highway and all airports in the state.

Arizona

Arizona Guide

www.arizonaguide.com

Greater Phoenix Convention & Visitors Bureau

www.phoenixcvb.com

Tucson Convention & Visitors Bureau

www.visittucson.org

Phoenix Sky Harbor International Airport

www.phxskyharbor.com/

Arkansas

Explore Arkansas

www.arkansas.com

California

California Division of Tourism
www.gocalif.ca.gov

California State Parks
www.cal-parks.ca.gov

Los Angeles Convention & Visitors Bureau
www.lacvb.com

Los Angeles International Airport – LAX
www.airports.ci.la.ca.us

San Francisco Convention & Visitors Bureau
www.sfvisitor.org

San Francisco International Airport
www.sfoairport.com

Napa Valley Conference & Visitors Bureau
www.napavalley.com

Lake Tahoe Visitors Authority
www.virtualtahoe.com

Ski California
www.skicalifornia.com

West Hollywood Convention & Visitors Bureau
www.visitwesthollywood.com

The Magic Kingdom – Walt Disney World
www.intercot.com/magickingdom/default/asp

Fun Plan – Avoid the crowds at Disneyland
www.funplans.com

Oakland International Airport

www.flyoakland.com

Colorado

Colorado Travel & Tourism Authority

www.colorado.com

Colorado Springs Convention & Visitors Bureau

www.coloradosprings-travel.com

Denver Colorado Convention & Visitors Bureau

www.denver.org

Denver International, Colorado

www.flydenver.com

Connecticut

Connecticut Tourism

www.tourism.state.ct.us

Delaware

State of Delaware Visitor Portal

www.delaware.gov/yahoo/Visitor

Florida

Visit Florida

www.flausa.com

Absolutely Florida

www.abfla.com

Daytona Beach Area Convention & Visitors Bureau

www.daytonabeachcvb.org

Palm Beach County

www.palmbeachfl.com

Emerald Coast Convention & Visitors Bureau

www.destin-fwb.com

Florida Keys & Key West Tourism

www.fla-keys.com/

Orlando County Convention & Visitors Bureau

www.go2orlando.com

Orlando International Airport

www.fcn.state.fl.us/goaa/

Greater Miami Convention & Visitors Bureau

www.miamiandbeaches.com

Miami Airport

www.miami-airport.com

Orlando Tampa International Airport

www.tampaairport.com

SeaWorld

www.seaworld.com

Wet 'n' Wild Adventure Park

www.wetnwild.com

Universal Studios

www.universalstudios.com

Kennedy Space Center

www.kennedyspacecenter.com

Georgia

Georgia On My Mind

www.gomm.com

Savannah Area Convention & Visitors Bureau

www.savannah-visit.com

Atlanta Convention & Visitors Bureau

www.acvb.com

Hartsfield Atlanta International Airport

http://atlanta-airport.com/

Hawaii

Hawaii Visitors & Convention Bureau

www.gohawaii.com

Hawaii Visitors Guide

www.global-town.com/vguide/hawaii.htm

Hawaii Airports

www.state.hi.us/dot/airports

Idaho

Discover Idaho

www.visitid.org

Illinois

Enjoy Illinois

www.enjoyillinois.com

Choose Chicago

www.chicago.il.org

Indiana

Enjoy Indiana
www.indianatourism.com

Iowa

Iowa Tourism
www.traveliowa.com

Kansas

Travelling in Kansas
www.kansascommerce.com/0400travel.html

Kentucky

Kentucky Tourism
www.kytourism.com

Louisville & Jefferson County Visitors Bureau
www.gotolouisville.com

Louisville International Airport
www.louintlairport.com/

Louisiana

Louisiana Travel
www.louisianatravel.com

New Orleans Visitors Bureau
www.neworleanscvb.com

New Orleans International Airport
www.flymsy.com

Maine

Visit Maine

www.visitmaine.com

Maryland

Welcome to Maryland

www.mdisfun.org

Baltimore Area Convention & Visitors Association

www.baltimore.org

Massachusetts

Welcome to Massachusetts

www.mass-vacation.com

Boston Online

www.boston-online.com/

Michigan

Travel Michigan

www.michigan.org

Great Lakes of North America

www.glna.org

Visit Detroit

www.visitdetroit.com

Detroit Metropolitan Airport

www.metroairport.com

Minnesota

Explore Minnesota

www.exploreminnesota.com

Mississippi

The South's Warmest Welcome to Mississippi

www.visitmississippi.org

Jackson Visitors Bureau

www.visitjackson.com

Jackson International Airport

www.jmaa.com/

Missouri

Missouri Tourism

www.missouritourism.org

Kansas City Visitors Bureau

www.visitkc.com

Kansas City International Airport

www.kcairports.com

Explore St Louis

www.st-louis-cvc.com

Lambert-St Louis International Airport

www.lambert-stlouis.com/

Montana

Discovering Montana

www.discoveringmontana.com

Nebraska

Visit Nebraska

www.visitnebraska.org

Nevada

NevadaTourism

www.travelnevada.com

Las Vegas Convention & Visitors Authority

www.lasvegas24hours.com

Welcome to Reno Lake Tahoe

www.playreno.com

Wet'n'Wild Adventure Park

www.wetnwild.com

New England

Visit New England

www.visitnewengland.com

New Hampshire

New Hampshire – The Road Less Travelled

www.visitnh.gov

New Jersey

New Jersey Tourism

www.state.nj.us/travel

Atlantic City Visitors Authority

www.atlanticcitynj.com

New Mexico

New Mexico Department of Tourism

www.newmexico.org

Santa Fe Visitors Bureau

www.santafe.org

Guide to Taos and Northern New Mexico

www.taoswebb.com

Albuquerque Visitors Bureau

www.abqcvb.org

Albuquerque International Sunport

www.cabq.gov/airport/index.html

New York

New York City Visitors Bureau

www.nycvisit.com

New York City Super Resource Guide

http://allny.com

New York.com

www.newyork.com

New York Today from The New York Times

www.newyorktoday.com

Long Island

www.licvb.com

Welcome to New York State

http://iloveny.state.ny.us

John F Kennedy International Airport

www.panynj.gov/aviation/jfkhomemain.html

North Carolina

Visit North Carolina

www.visitnc.com

Raleigh-Durham International Airport

www.rdu.com

North Dakota

North Dakota Travel and Tourism

www.ndtourism.com

Ohio

Ohio Tourism

www.ohiotourism.com

Oklahoma

Oklahoma Native America

www.travelok.com

Oregon

Travel Oregon

www.traveloregon.com

Portland Oregon Visitors Association

www.pova.com

Pennsylvania

Pure Pennsylvania

www.visit.state.pa.us

Gettysburg

www.gettysburg.com

Greater Philadelphia Tourism

www.gophila.com

Rhode Island

Rhode Island Tourism

www.visitrhodeisland.com

Newport Visitors Bureau

www.gonewport.com/

South Carolina

South Carolina Tourism Office

www.travelsc.com

Charleston Visitors Bureau

www.charlestoncvb.com

South Dakota

South Dakota Department of Tourism

www.travelsd.com

Rapid City Visitors Bureau

www.rapidcitycvb.com

Sioux Falls Tourism

www.siouxfalls.org

Tennessee

Tennessee Tourism

www.state.tn.us/tourism/country.html

Nashville Visitors Bureau

www.nashvillecvb.com/

Nashville International Airport

www.nashintl.com/

IntroMemphis: An Insider's Guide

www.intromemphis.com

Graceland

www.elvis.com/graceland/

Memphis International Airport

www.mscaa.com/

Dolly Parton's Smoky Mountain Theme Park

www.dollywood.com

Texas

Texas Tourism

www.traveltex.com

Dallas Visitors Bureau

www.dallascvb.com

Fort Worth Visitors Bureau

www.fortworth.com

Dallas/Fort Worth International Airport

www.dfwairport.com/

El Paso Visitors Bureau

www.elpasocvb.com

Official Guide to Houston

www.houston-guide.com

Houston Airport System

www.houstonairportsystem.org

Utah

Utah.com

www.utah.com

Welcome to Salt Lake City

www.ci.slc.ut.us

Vermont

Visit Vermont

www.visit-vermont.com

Vermont Tourist Information

www.vermont.org

Virginia

Virginia.org

www.virginia.org

Washington DC

The Official Tourism Website of Washington DC

www.washington.org

DC Online

www.washdc.org

Metropolitan Washington Airports Authority

www.metwashairports.com

Washington State

Washington State Tourism

www.tourism.wa.gov

Seattle Visitors Bureau

www.seeseattle.org

Seattle-Tacoma International Airport

www.portseattle.org./seatac/

West Virginia

West Virginia – Wild and Wonderful

www.state.wv.us/tourism

Wisconsin

Travel Wisconsin

www.travelwisconsin.com

Milwaukee Visitors Bureau

www.milwaukee.org

Wyoming

Wyoming Tourism

www.wyomingtourism.org

Jackson Hole – Get Further Away

www.jacksonhole.com

URUGUAY

Uraguay

www.planetlatino.net/uraguay.htm
There is very little information on Uraguay (in English) available on the net. This site offers some basic background.

UZBEKISTAN

Destination Uzbekistan

www.lonelyplanet.com/destinations/central_asia/uzbekistan
Lonely Planet's reliable guide to Uzbekistan, home to some of the oldest towns in the world and some of the main centres of the Silk Road.

VANUATU

Welcome to Vanuatu

www.vanuatutourism.com
The official site for the Pacific island, with details on activities and local customs.

VATICAN CITY

Vatican: The Holy See

www.vatican.va
Slightly impenetrable site, but amongst the details on the rituals and the Swiss Guards is some information on the museums and a map or two.

VENEZUELA

Venezuela Yours

www.venezuelatuya.com/tour/toureng.htm
Rather noisy site providing a whistle-stop tour of the country.

VIETNAM

Vietnam Tourism

www.vietnamtourism.com
Official overview, with information on the cities, provinces and people.

Vietnam Travel City

www.vietnamtraveling.com/main.html
Assorted links to information about Vietnam.

YEMEN

Yemen

www.mideastravelnet.com/mideastsite/yemen/cs.htm
Brief, basic facts on history, cities, sights and travel in Yemen.

YUGOSLAVIA

Serbia

www.serbia-tourism.org
Official site with details of all the natural attractions, cities, villages and culture to be found in Serbia.

Visit Montenegro

www.visit-montenegro.com
Detailed site, taking a look at beaches, events, art and culture and all things Montenegran, with some good links.

ZAMBIA

Zambia: A Complete Travel Guide

www.africa-insites.com/zambia/travel/index.htm
As the name suggests, this site leaves no Zambian stone unturned and covers all the attractions and practical travel tips in depth.

ZIMBABWE

Zimbabwe Tourism Authority

www.tourismzimbabwe.co.zw
A look at the natural wonders and wildlife, plenty of facts and information for travellers, but little on politics or current events.

DEPENDENCIES OF THE WORLD

AMERICAN SAMOA

American Samoa Office of Tourism

www.amsamoa.com
America's South Pacific Polynesian paradise – the map, the history, the language and customs plus plenty of practical information.

ANGUILLA

The Anguilla Guide

http://net.ai
Dive in for information on beaches, activities, nightlife, restaurants, festivals and current events in Anguilla.

Anguilla Online Tourist Guide

www.turq.com/anguilla
Getting there, staying there – and a photo album to dream on.

ARUBA

Aruba Online

www.olmco.com/aruba/
Tips and travel planning, restaurant reservations, weather forecasts, sample taxi fares, and an events calendar including carnival.

Welcome to Aruba

www.aruba.com
Folklore and traditions, medical facilities, where to eat, caves and churches, nightlife and butterfly farms – and a virtual tour map.

BRITISH VIRGIN ISLANDS

BVI Welcome

www.bviwelcome.com
Interactive, electronic magazine produced in collaboration with the BVI tourist board. Background information and specifics on dining, shops and services.

British Virgin Islands – Online Travel Guide

www.b-v-i.com
The beaches, the nightlife, the food, and an entertaining virtual tour of the islands.

CAYMAN ISLANDS

Cayman Islands Department of Tourism

www.caymanislands.ky
Culture, heritage, things to do, individual island reports, plenty of useful information – bar the not-very-interactive interactive maps.

FALKLAND ISLANDS

Falklands Islands Tourist Board

www.tourism.org.fk
Basic facts about travelling in these remote, beautiful islands.

FRENCH GUIANA

Destination French Guiana

www.lonelyplanet.com/destinations/south_america/french_guiana/

Impeccable attention to detail from Lonely Planet - everything from health risks to cultural background.

FRENCH POLYNESIA

French Polynesia

www.polynesianislands.com/fp
Facts on the islands that make up Polynesian paradise: Tahiti, Moorea, Bora Bora, Huahine and all the others.

Tahiti Tourisme

www.tahiti-tourisme.com
A myriad of useful facts about the islands, taking in the history, culture, attractions, pearls, diving and much more.

GIBRALTAR

Gibraltar Home Page

www.gibraltar.gi/tourism
What to see, and where to eat and drink on the Rock.

GUADELOUPE

Destination Guadeloupe

www.lonelyplanet.com/destinations/caribbean/guadeloupe/
Full of facts for travellers to this French Caribbean island.

GUAM

Welcome to Guam

www.visitguam.org
Things to do and what to see on this American Pacific island.

MARTINIQUE

Martinique

http://www.touristmartinique.com

Brightly coloured site offers a brief and tempting guide to Martinique – attractions, festivals, celebrations, restaurants.

MONTSERRAT

Visit Montserrat

www.visitmontserrat.com
General information on the island, what to do and where to avoid (the exclusion zone caused by volcanic eruptions).

NETHERLAND ANTILLES

Info Bonaire

www.infobonaire.com
The official Bonaire website includes including diving and snorkelling, restaurants, travel tips and island news.

Curacao Tourist Board

www.curacao-tourism.com
An overview of the beautiful beaches, plus information on the nitty-gritty – visas, climate, what to pack, taxi fare and tipping.

Saba Tourist Bureau

www.turq.com/saba
General and travel information on this Dutch Caribbean island.

St Eustatius Tourist Office

www.turq.com/statia
The official round up of delights and advice for visitors to the Caribbean island known locally as Statia.

Welcome to St Maarten

www.st-maarten.com
Shared by two separate governments, St Maarten has a dual French and Dutch heritage. This site looks at the attractions in both French and British parts of the island – and has all the practical information too.

New Caledonia

Tourism Council of the South Pacific

www.tcsp.com
Click on 'Destinations' and follow the links for New Caledonia.

New Caledonia Tourism

www.new-caledonia-tourism.nc
Practical tips about money and banks, language, health and vaccinations, as well as some evocative destinational information.

Northern Mariana Islands

Marianas Visitors Authority

www.visit-marianas.com/
Interactive maps, travel tips and an event calendar.

Reunion

Réunion

www.la-reunion-tourisme.com/Adefault.htm
The official site, complete with all the enticing information necessary for a visit to this French island in the Indian Ocean.

Turks & Caicos

Welcome to Turks & Caicos

www.turksandcaicostourism.com
A good look at marine and island life on this extensive coral reef.

US Virgin Islands

US Virgin Islands Department of Tourism

www.usvi.org/tourism
The official guide to these incredibly popular islands.

Chapter 3: **Preparing your trip** ❧

by Jonathan Lorie

WEATHER REPORTS

BBC Weather Centre

www.bbc.co.uk/weather
Excellent summaries of typical weather patterns country-by-country, plus forecasts on the even the most obscure towns.

CNN Weather

www.cnn.com/weather/index.html
Good but brief forecasts for most towns worldwide.

Yahoo Weather

http://weather.yahoo.com
Current weather and five-day forecasts, searchable by cities of the world. Links to excellent graphics – maps, charts, even videos.

WEXAS

www.wexas.com
Unusual and useful data on rainy seasons and sea temperatures, plus quick country guides (temperature, humidity, rainfall) in the 'Traveller's Handbook/Directory' section.

British Meteorological Office

www.meto.gov.uk
Official government weather department's site. Good on Britain, sketchy on 'abroad'.

Hurricane Watch

www.jgds.com/hurricane
Promising site under construction: currently useful for the USA.

Snow and Avalanche Centre

www.csac.org
Groovy non-profit website, featuring curiosities such as an avalanche map of the world. Quite useful reports on many snow areas.

World Meteorological Organization

www.wmo.ch
Solemn reports on scientific issues from the UN's weather agency.

Rain or Shine

www.rainorshine.com/
Hourly forecasts for over 43,000 cities worldwide.

HEALTH ISSUES

WEXAS

www.wexas.com
Advice on foreign diseases, plus vaccination guides and health profiles for every country, in the 'Traveller's Healthbook' section.

Lonely Planet

www.lonelyplanet.com/health/
As snappy and helpful as you'd expect from the guidebook giant. Easy to use and fun to visit.

MASTA

www.masta.org.uk
Very reliable information from the non-profit organisation Medical Advisory Services for Travellers Abroad.

Centers for Disease Control and Prevention

www.cdc.gov/travel
Excellent practical information provided by the US government's official agency for disease control.

British Government

www.doh.gov.uk/traveladvice
Official advice for travellers, including immunisation guides and payment advice.

Travel Health Online

www.tripprep.com
Detailed health information for every country in the world.

International Society of Travel Medicine

www.istm.org
Excellent reports on disease outbreaks around the world, and other adventurous topics.

Red Cross

www.ifrc.org
Directory of Red Cross and Red Crescent Societies worldwide.

World Health Organisation

www.who.int
Heavyweight medical information on global health issues and politics. Also medical journals and 'Disease Outbreak News'.

24DrTravel.com

www.24drtravel.com
General and country-specific travel advice, dispensed by British GPs. Offers online consultations while you're abroad (for a fee).

Travel Health

www.travelhealth.co.uk
Calls itself a 'nurse-led website'. Covers sensible range of practical medical issues.

Tropical Screening

www.tropicalscreening.com
Commercial site offering online advice while you are abroad plus clinical service when you return. Run by seriously experienced travelling doctors.

Third World Traveler

www.thirdworldtraveler.com/Travel/TravelHealth.html
Right-on site covering adventurous destinations – and the health issues therein. Great quotes from the giants of history.

Virtual Hospital

www.vh.org
Fascinating concept: an archive of medical information dressed up as an online hospital, run by medics at the University of Iowa. Claims to receive six million hits a month.

Internet Health Library

www.internethealthlibrary.com
Somewhat alternative approach to health issues.

Healthy Flying

www.flyana.com
Sparky individual website by Diana Fairechild, who describes herself as a consumer activist. Views on all kinds of travel health issues, especially related to flying.

Disability World

www.disabilityworld.com
News, reports, travel ideas and good links page.

Access-Able

http://www.access-able.com
Well-meaning but clunky site on disability travel. Claims to offer country-by-country information on facilities and services.

PERSONAL SAFETY

WEXAS

www.wexas.com
Section on 'Global Hotspots' surveys the world's troublespots for travellers, plus articles on safety issues in 'Traveller' section.

World's Most Dangerous Places

www.fieldingtravel.com

Background information on hazardous countries. Comprehensive if not always up to date.

US Government Travel Warnings

www.travel.state.gov/travel_warnings.html
Comprehensive if a little cautious, official warnings on dangerous countries.

Judicial Assistance

www.travel.state.gov/judicial_assistance.html
Very thorough information on legal process around the world – and how to get legal help.

UK Foreign Office

www.fco.gov.uk/travel
The official UK site for travel warnings: has been criticised as over-cautious and out of date.

Third World Traveler

www.thirdworld.traveler.com
Streetwise website on travel in the developing world.

NOLO

www.nolo.com/encyclopedia/ctim_ency.html
Self-help law site offering advice on keeping clear of the law around the world.

ABC News

abcnews.go.com/sections/world/dp/dp_intro.html
Riveting if weird reports and links on unsavoury parts of the world.

Street Scams of Barcelona

www.jones.tc/barna/scams.html
Highly individual but convincing account of various things to avoid, from one Terry Jones (not, apparently, the Monty Python comedy star).

Real World Rescue

www.realworldrescue.com
Professional security firm offering detailed if undigested reports on global risk areas.

Airsafe

www.airsafe.com
Fascinating collection of terrifying air travel data, such as 'Fatal events (by region)' and 'Selected accidents (celebrities)'.

Airline Safety

www.airlinesafety.com
Guerrilla website hosting provocative debates on safety issues, with a bias against the air companies and regulators.

Airline Quality

www.airlinequality.com
Awards 'star' ratings to airlines, plus air industry news and gossip.

RED TAPE

World Travel Guide

www.travel-guides.com
Country-by-country information gives lengthy details on visas and duty free allowances.

WEXAS

www.wexas.com
'Country profiles' area in 'Traveller's Handbook' section lists duty-free allowances, visa requirements and embassy addresses.

Embassy World

www.embassyworld.com
Searchable database of embassy contact details worldwide.

British Foreign Office

www.fco.gov.uk/links.asp
Searchable listing of British diplomatic missions overseas, plus various international bodies.

Embassy Web

www.embassyweb.com
Still being constructed, but looks to become an interesting mix of useful information (embassy addresses etc.), viewers' opinions and FAQs on various aspects of the diplomatic world.

Tourist Offices Worldwide

www.towd.com
Listed by destination, plus useful links to various country and destination sites.

Association of National Tourist Offices in the UK

www.antor.com
Contact details for foreign tourist boards in Britain, with good links to their countries' other websites.

UK Passport Agency

www.ukpa.gov.uk
Online applications for passports, plus information on procedures.

The Visa Service

www.visaservice.co.uk
Commercial site offering to obtain visas for individual travellers or for companies.

Work Permit

www.visa-free.com
Commercial service procuring work permits in UK, USA and some European countries.

MAPS

Oddens

http://oddens.geog.uu.nl/index.html
Excellent starting point, contains 14,000 links to other map sites. Easy viewing, too. Run by the University of Utrecht, bless 'em.

International Map Trade Organisation

www.maptrade.org/links.html
Very useful site listing members of this trade association all over the world, who specialise in all kinds of cartographic products.

WEXAS

www.wexas.com
Look out for the detailed advice on 'Choosing Maps' (in 'Traveller's handbook/Logistics/Researching your trip').

Map World

www.map-guides.com
Good site for buying maps. Easy to use, rapid searching, good selection includes fairly obscure places.

Stanfords

www.stanfords.co.uk
Claims to be 'the world's finest map shop', now online. Thorough range of maps to buy, which you find via the 'Country' selection.

Maps Worldwide

www.mapsworldwide.co.uk
Commercial site for ordering maps from many publishers. Useful global selection, though best on UK: you can order Ordnance Survey maps here. Good links to other country-information sources.

Map Quest

www.mapquest.com
Presents good clear maps, even on remote countries, in a well structured site.

About Geography

http://geography.miningco.com/science/geography/library/maps/blindex.html
Good maps, good links, easy to access. Annoying advertisements, but otherwise recommended.

National Geographic

www.nationalgeographic.com/resources/ngo/maps
You may have more luck than we did with this site, which promises all kinds of fascinating sections but takes an age to download.

Atlapedia

www.atlapedia.com
Allows you to view maps, though they are rather large scale. Provides good and detailed information on each country's politics, history, climate etc.

World Atlas

www.worldatlas.com/aatlas/world.htm
Fairly basic but easy-to-find maps of most but not all countries.

Metro Planet

www.metropla.net/
Quick access to subway maps of cities worldwide.

US Naval Observatory

http://aa.usno.navy.mil/aa/faq/docs/world_tzones.html
World timezone map.

UK Hydrographic Office

www.ukho.gov.uk
World's leading provider of marine charts. Site currently under construction, but worth checking for progress.

GPS World

www.gpsworld.com
Magazine site on issues relating to Global Positioning Systems technology, plus buyer's guide.

Royal Geographic Society

www.rgs.org
You can purchase original historic maps from past expeditions, via the section on 'Collections/Map room'. A curiosity for collectors.

Streetmap

www.streetmap.co.uk
Type in a UK postcode for a detailed map of surrounding streets.

RAC

www.rac.co.uk/services/routeplanner
Will calculate routes and provide road maps for journeys between major European towns.

BOOKS

WEXAS

www.wexas.com
Wide-ranging and authoritative reviews of top travel books past and present are in 'Recommended Reading', arranged by continent ('Traveller's Handbook/Directory/Preparing your Trip').

Booksellers

Stanfords

www.stanfords.co.uk
The world's largest travel bookshop is now online. Extensive range of travel books and maps in an easy-to-access format.

The Travel Bookshop

www.thetravelbookshop.co.uk
Online arm of one of Britain's oldest travel bookstores. Good specialist selection.

Adventurous Traveler

www.adventuroustraveler.com/
Rather impressive selection of books for hardcore travel and activity fiends – nice write-ups, good search facility.

The Book Place

www.thebookplace.co.uk
Offers intelligent and lengthy reviews of a wide-range of books. Not a specialist travel site, but very good on searching by relevant keywords.

Amazon

www.amazon.co.uk
Mainstream book site with a very mainstream travel section.

Alphabet Street

www.alphabetstreet.infront.co.uk
Ditto.

BOL

www.bol.com
The travel section of this site seems to be a front for The Travel Bookshop, a well-established store that deserves your custom more directly (see above).

Talking Books

www.talkingbooks.co.uk
Selection of books on tape and CD, including travel section.

Maps Worldwide

www.mapsworldwide.com
Sells maps and guidebooks from across the globe.

Guidebooks

WEXAS

www.wexas.com

Contains a library of guidebooks from Lonely Planet, Rough Guides and Columbus. Also check 'A guide to guidebooks' in the 'Traveller's Handbook' section for interesting qualitative advice.

Lonely Planet

www.lonelyplanet.co.uk
Grandaddy of guidebook publishers, with a site that's bang up to date. Offers excerpts from their own books, plus lots of extras. Especially useful are updates available at www.lonelyplanet.com/upgrades which you can download and keep. Best for backpackers.

Footprint Handbooks

www.footprintbooks.com
Innovative and in-depth, an independent publisher offering thoughtful guidebooks that are increasingly authoritative.

Bradmans

www.bradmans.com
Excellent information for business travellers, focusing on major cities worldwide.

Fielding

www.fieldingtravel.com/df
Publishers of The World's Most Dangerous Places, a cult guide that is reflected faithfully online – edgy, provocative, hard core and just a little out of date.

Rough Guides

www.roughguides.com
Over 3,500 destinations on a database, plus a related e-zine with in-depth articles and travel tips. Good reading for the rougher traveller.

Time Out

www.timeout.com
Insider coverage of various popular cities, mostly in Europe and USA. Includes entertainment guides, and some ability to book tickets for events.

Dorling Kindersley

www.travel.dk.com/uk
First-rate site reflecting the excellence of their printed books. Essential guides to a slightly limited range of cities.

Frommers

www.frommers.com
If you like the books you'll like the site. What else can we say?

Fodors

www.fodors.com
Upmarket if a little safe. The site allows you to create and print out mini-guides and your own itineraries based on destination and budget.

Let's Go

www.letsgo.com
Largely incomprehensible site claiming to suit the budget and student traveller.

Moon Handbooks

www.moon.com
Mainly an ordering service for their highly individualistic backpacker guides.

Booktailor.com

www.booktailor.com
A brilliant concept, this site enables the user to create and print out their own guidebook, using information chosen from respected publishers such as Lonely Planet and Footprint Handbooks. The list of destinations is not exhaustive, but is increasing.

Dictionaries & Translators

Travlang

www.travlang.com
Wide range of free online dictionaries, plus book-ordering facility.

Free Translation

www.freetranslation.com
Instantaneous onscreen translation of your words and phrases.

Berlitz

www.berlitz.com
Ordering facility for language books and courses from the market leader.

Babel Fish

http://babel.altavista.com
Instantaneous onscreen translation of your words and phrases.

Linguaphone

www.linguaphone.com
Linguaphone pioneered the concept of self-study language teaching. This site has information on their products and online courses.

TRAVEL JOURNALISM

Publications

Traveller

www.traveller.org.uk
Oldest UK travel magazine – and still a heavyweight. Not to be confused with 'Condé Nast Traveller' (see below). Publishes long features and opinions on adventurous and authentic journeys.

National Geographic

www.nationalgeographic.com
Best-known travel magazine in the world, with pictures and text to match. Top quality stuff.

Salon

www.salon.com./travel
Wanderlust section of this online magazine used to contain some top travel journalism – now accessible through an archive search.

New York Times

www.nytimes.com/pages/travel
Register here to read some classic travel writing.

Condé Nast Traveller

www.cntraveller.com
The glamour-seeker's bible. High-quality articles on the high life abroad.

Wanderlust

www.wanderlust.co.uk
Backpacker's bible: useful and inspiring articles on offbeat and mainstream destinations for independent travellers of all ages.

Sunday Times

www.sunday-times.co.uk
Good travel section with consumer articles and advice from UK national newspaper.

Holiday Which

www.which.net/holiday/contents.html
Excellent selection of destination reviews, plus a wealth of other consumer information.

CNN Traveller

www.cnntraveller.com
Online travel magazine, with assorted articles and country facts from the American news organisation.

Getaway

www.getawaytoafrica.com
Online version of top South African travel magazine, specialising in adventure and wildlife articles.

Explore

www.explore-mag.com
Intrepid Canadian magazine site featuring adventure travel worldwide.

Travel Intelligence

www.travelintelligence.com
Fascinating site based on travel writing of high quality. Includes the entertaining section 'Before you die', where users nominate their favourite destination – and explain why.

South American Explorers Club

www.samexplo.org
Hardcore travellers' club offering useful trip reports and contacts.

Professional writers and photographers

British Guild of Travel Writers

www.bgtw.org
Not terribly interactive site, but useful for accessing this influential trade association and network.

National Union of Journalists

www.gn.apc.org/media/flindex.html
Trade magazine for freelancers.

Journalist.net

www.journalist.net
Information exchange for journalists, especially good for picking up on the PR industry and its opportunities.

Travel Writers

www.travelwriters.com
Useful US-based site for freelancers.

Food, wine and travel

www.ifwtwa.org

International association of food, wine and travel writers.

Society of American Travel Writers

www.satw.org
Membership association.

Royal Photographic Society

www.rps.org
Member association with a useful travel photography division.

PhotoPro

www.photopro.co.uk
Step-by-step advice for photographers building their own websites.

Shutter Chances

www.shutterchances.com.au
Photographic club organising field trips in Africa, Australia, Japan and New Zealand.

TRAVELOGUES, CHATSITES & NEWSGROUPS

These sites come and go very fast, depending on the enthusiasm and finances of the organisers. Their quality can also change rapidly, especially if they are not kept up to date. At time of press, the most interesting ones are as follows:

Travelogues and chatsites

WEXAS

www.wexas.com
'Travel Talk' section allows you to email your questions to celebrity travellers or travel experts.

Travelmag

www.travelmag.co.uk

*Entertaining and eclectic site featuring adventurous travellers'
views and useful snippets of information.*

Rec.Travel Library

www.travel-library.com
*Links to travelogues and reports for nearly every country in the
world.*

eTravel

www.etravel.org
Friendly backpacker site aiming to help the first-time traveller.

Tips 4 Trips

www.tips4trips.com
*Entertaining and potentially useful tips from fellow travellers on
all kinds of topics.*

Travel Donkey

www.traveldonkey.com
*Nice idea but patchy content. The concept is an interactive site
where travellers can publish their own stories. The 'Live Diaries'
section is lively, the 'Travelogues' section disappointing.*

Terra Quest

www.terraquest.com
Virtual video tours of some parts of the world.

Art of Travel

www.artoftravel.com
*Apparently a self-published guide to backpacking the world on $25
a day.*

Caribbean Travel Round-up

www.caribtravelnews.com
A mix of tourism news and visitors' experiences.

The Travelzine

http://thetravelzine.com

Quirky self-published travellers' tales from Toronto retirees Don and Linda Freedman, your hosts to world adventure.

Travel Experiences

www.travel-experiences.com
Backpacker forum featuring noticeboards and travelogues.

The Virtual Tourist

www.vtourist.com
Eclectic membership site where real travellers share their experiences. Good links to other country-based information.

Locals In The Know

www.localsintheknow.com
Click on a country to see entries from the people who know it best – the local residents. Not every country has an entry, but where people have written about their home town, the information is worth noting if you're planning a visit.

Newsgroups

The sites listed below are recommended newsgroups. You won't find them on the web, but they are accessible via a newsgroup client (such as Freeagent) or a website such as www.dejanews.com. For example, if you go to www.dejanews.com (recently absorbed into the Googly search engine), it will open many newsgroups and related links for you.

Content and quality in newsgroups varies enormously, depending on who's posting what messages, so they are impossible to review here. You'll just have to form your own judgement. But they may be useful if you have a question that no one else has answered.

alt.travel
alt.travel.uk.air
rec.travel.africa
alt.travel.canada
alt.travel.eurail.youth-hostels

alt.travel.uk.marketplace
alt.travel.ideas
rec.travel.budget.backpack
rec.travel.usa-canada
rec.travel.misc
rec.travel.australia
rec.travel.latin-america
rec.travel.europe
rec.travel.caribbean
alt.travel.roadtrip

CYBERCAFÉS

Cybercafés

www.cybercafes.com
Easy-to-use site that lists 4,000 cafés worldwide.

Cybercafe Search Engine

www.cybercaptive.com
Simple access to café addresses worldwide.

EQUIPMENT

Wexas

www.wexas.com
A whole section devoted to advice on 'What to Take' – specialist clothing, food on the move, lightweight gear, the ultimate kitlist (in 'Traveller's Handbook/Logistics').

Outdoor gear

Field and Trek

www.field-trek.co.uk
Equipment and clothing for all kinds of outdoor and adventurous activities.

Blacks

www.blacks.co.uk
Online shopping at major UK outdoor clothing and gear shop.

Snow and Rock

www.snowandrock.com
Groovy but serious gear suppliers.

Nomad

www.nomadtravel.co.uk
Good range of serious outdoor gear and clothing.

Brasher Boot Co

www.brasher.co.uk
Leading brand of hiking boots.

Berghaus

www.berghaus.com
High performance technical clothing for serious outdoor pursuits.

Cotswold Camping

www.cotswold-outdoor.com
Wide range of camping gear.

Penrith Survival Equipment

www.edirectory.co.uk/penrithsurvival/index.htm
Serious gear for extreme activities.

Rohan

www.rohan.co.uk
Leading suppliers of outdoor clothing.

YHA

www.yhaadventure.com
Site under construction, from major outdoor gear supplier.

LL Bean

www.llbean.com
Celebrated US supplier of fashionable outdoor clothes and gear.

Ellis Brigham

www.ellis-brigham.com
Leading mountain sports supplier.

9 Feet

www.9feet.com
Up-and-coming outdoor gear supplier.

Ski Surf

www.skisurf.co.uk
Long-established supplier for surf and snow enthusiasts.

Typhoon

www.typhoon-int.co.uk
Extensive range of watersports equipment.

Ski Stop Warehouse

www.skistop.com/skclose.htm
Big US retailer for snowsports gear, including discounted items.

Adventure Sports Online

www.adventuresports.com/new/shopdir.htm
Good outdoor gear from a variety of suppliers in the USA.

Aqua Flite

http://aquaflite.com
Specialists in wetsuits and other diving gear.

Aquatic Outfitters

http://aquaticoutfitters.com

Good range of mainstream watersports gear.

Cumberland Transit

www.ctransit.com
Outdoor gear retailer in Tennessee: flyfishing and whitewater rafting, plus the usual hiking stuff.

Leki

www.leki.com
Hard-core equipment from the USA.

Lightweight Gear Shop

www.backpacking.net/gearshop.html
Ultra-light equipment, mostly for camping.

Long Road Travel Supplies

www.longroad.com
Specialises in portable mosquito nets, bednets and sleeping bags.

Mountain Woman

www.mountainwoman.com
Gear and clothing for women adventurers.

Northwest River Supplies

www.nrscatalog.com
Small craft and boating equipment.

Overtons

www.overtons.com
Claims to be the world's largest watersports dealer.

Savanna Jones

www.savannajones.com
Off-road vehicles and parts.

Tilley

www.tilley.com
Fashion clothing with an adventure twist.

Gear Head

www.gearhd.com
Highly personalised service sourcing your required adventure gear.

Gearoom

www.gearoom.com
Hardcore adventure gear, reviewed sensibly.

Photographic supplies

Jessops

www.jessops.co.uk
Leading retailer of camera equipment, now online. Their website lists 20,000 products.

Ilford

www.ilford.com/html/us_english/homeng.html
Professional quality photographic products.

Colab

www.colab.co.uk
Good range of camera products, plus laboratory services – including sophisticated electronic facilities.

Camera Care Systems

www.ccscentre.co.uk
Protective cases and other carrying systems for cameras, including for extreme conditions.

Tamrac

www.tamrac.com
Ditto.

Jono

www.jonomailorder.co.uk
UK retailer of discounted camera film and batteries.

Camera makers

Agfa

www.agfa.co.uk

Canon

www.canon.co.uk

Fuji

www.fuji.co.uk

Kodak

www.kodak.co.uk

Minolta

www.minolta.co.uk

Pentax

www.pentax.co.uk

Olympus

www.olympus.co.uk

Medical kit

Nomad

www.nomadtravel.co.uk
Wide range of travel health products.

MASTA

www.masta.org.uk
The non-profit Medical Advisory Services for Travellers Abroad, set up by the London School of Hygiene and Tropical Medicine.

BCB

www.bcb.ltd.uk
Well-established firm supplying custom-made products.

Travel with Care

www.travelwithcare.co.uk
First aid and dental kits, water purification equipment, insect repellents and mosquito nets are all available from this online shop.

Luggage and security

Wexas

www.wexas.com
Members' site offering special 'passepartout' service for holding secure information online, in case of loss.

Discount Luggage

www.luggageman.com
As it says. Based in USA.

Eagle Creek

www.eaglecreek.com
Groovy luggage site.

Cencal Aviation Products

www.cencal.com
Flight bags and other accessories originally designed for the aviation industry using extra strong materials.

Luggage Land

www.luggageland.com.au
Australian site, amusingly presented.

Samsonite

www.samsonite-europe.com
Well-known luggage brand.

Mulberry

www.mulberry-england.co.uk/collections/luggage
Classy luggage brand.

Letravelstore

www.letravelstore.com
Fairly good mainstream selection of luggage and accessories.

Yellowtag

www.yellowtag.com
Global lost-and-found system.

Catch 22

www.catch22products.co.uk
Funky site selling travel security products.

Travelite

www.travelite.org
Advice and FAQs on luggage issues.

Information technology

Teleadapt

www.teleadapt.com
Retailer specialising in mobile connectivity: good for advice and products.

Mobal

www.mobalrental.com
Rent mobile phones for abroad, or see if yours will work out there.

FINANCE

Travelex

www.travelex.co.uk
Good site from Britain's largest foreign exchange company. Here you can order foreign currency to be delivered to your home, or simply find the conversion rates for world currencies.

WEXAS

www.wexas.com
Advice on organising your finances and choosing insurance (in 'Traveller's Handbook/Logistics/Support Sysytems'), plus facility for ordering insurance online.

MasterCard

www.mastercard.com/atm
Global ATM locator for MasterCard, Maestro and Cirrus cards.

Visa

www.visa.com/pd/atm/main.html
Global ATM-locator for Visa cards.

Exchange rates

www.x-rates.com
Onscreen currency convertor.

Universal Currency Converter

www.xe.net/currency
Ditto.

Global Refund

www.globalrefund.com
Where and how to get refunds on VAT when buying abroad.

Ed and Julie

www.twenj.com/moneyand.htm
Financial travel advice from self-styled experts Ed and Julie.

CONSUMER ISSUES

Consumer association

www.which.net

Very useful for advice and research into all kinds of consumer issues, including travel – with plenty of destination reviews.

Holiday Complaints

www.holidaycomplaint.com
Interesting forum where holidaymakers can publish complaints against travel companies, and – maybe – the companies will reply. More usefully, you can read about the problems other people have had, and avoid them. Still under development, this site ought to become compulsive reading – eg 'Dirty, noisy, disgusting food, don't go there.'

Holiday Travel Watch

www.holidaytravelwatch.com
Consumer rights site, currently offering general advice and hoping to carry detailed reports on destinations in the near future.

Air Travel Organiser's Licence

www.atol.org.uk
Website of the air industry body that regulates consumer protection for flights and air holidays. Contains some useful information on your statutory rights.

SOCIAL CONTACTS

Globetrotters

www.globetrotters.co.uk
Informal and sparky membership club for independent travellers. There are over 1,000 Globetrotters worldwide, happy to network, exchange information, source accommodation and even find travelling companions.

Lonely Planet Thorn Tree

http://thorntree.lonelyplanet.com/thorn/branches.pl

This popular bulletin board on the Lonely Planet site is a good place to look for potential travel companions.

Travel Talk – Rough Guides

http://travel.roughguides.com/talk/
Post a message here to talk travel, get advice and to make contact with other travellers.

South American Explorers Club

www.samexplo.org
A good source of information about South and Central America, and a point of contact for travellers interested in this part of the world.

Yahoo Clubs, Travel

http://dir.clubs.yahoo.com/Recreation_Sports/Travel/
Companion_Services/
Links to a variety of Yahoo's travel clubs can be found on this page – from a club for women who would like to find female travelling companions, and contacts for people who don't want or like to travel alone.

The Travel Companion Network

www.travel-companion.net/
Search for a suitable travel companion by browsing the categorised lists or by placing an advertisement.

Travel Chums

www.travelchums.com
Matches up like-minded travellers.

Passport Will Travel

www.passportwilltravel.com
Join up (for a monthly fee) and find a fellow member to travel with.

Chapter 4: **While you're there** ❧

by Amy Sohanpaul

FOOD AND DRINK

Many of the country websites listed in Chapter 2 have detailed information on local restaurants, entertainment and culture. The sites listed below offer additional advice on having a good time abroad.

GLOBAL WEBSITES

Via Michelin

www.michelin-travel.com
Amidst the general travel information is a list of recommended restaurants in Europe and France, and a magazine which has food and drink related articles. The address for this site is set to change to www.viamichelin.com.

Restaurant Row

www.restaurantrow.com
Information on over 100,000 restaurants in over 7,000 towns and cities worldwide. Calls itself 'The World's Largest Dining Guide'.

Chef Moz

www.chefmoz.dmoz.org
Over 50,000 restaurants from around the world are listed on this site, some have been reviewed, in other cases there are links to reviews. Despite the number of restaurants, coverage tends to be uneven – some countries have no entries, others have dozens.

WEXAS

www.wexas.com
Library of worldwide guidebooks from Lonely Planet, Rough Guides and Columbus.

Fodors

www.fodors.com/reviews/drevselect.cfm

Reviews of restaurants in favourite Fodor destinations, from Amsterdam to Washington; and in every continent, although the longest listings are for Europe and America.

Time Out

www.timeout.com
Restaurants, bars, nightlife, culture, arts and entertainment in over 30 international cities, from 'The World's Living Guide'.

Zagat

www.zagat.com
The online version of the reliable guidebooks, with reviews of over 20,000 restaurants. Most of these are in the USA, the others are in London, Paris, Tokyo, Toronto and Vancouver.

Wine & Dine

www.winedine.co.uk
Bills itself as 'The electronic magazine for lovers of wine, food and travel'. An eclectic collection of articles on all three, with some overlap – a wine guide to France, reviews of restaurants in major cities in Europe, the USA and some from further afield.

Global Destinations

www.globalgourmet.com/destinations
Choose a country and check out the cuisine – this site isn't full of restaurant reviews but does offer useful culinary background to countries around the world.

Food Tourist

www.foodtourist.com
Searchable database of restaurants in Europe, Australia, the USA and South-East Asia.

The Sushi World Guide

www.sushi.infogate.de
A guide to Japanese restaurants outside Japan, a glossary of sushi terms and links to other sushi sites.

Chinese Cuisine

http://chinesefood.about.com/msub04.htm
Links to Chinese restaurants around the world, and some interesting articles about the different strands of Chinese cuisine, including a look at the history of dim sum.

Eat Jamaican

http://eatjamaican.com/
A guide to Jamaican eateries around the world.

Decanter

www.decanter.com
A classy, cultured site, offering the route to good wine from all over the world, and selected international restaurants too.

Veg Dining

www.vegdining.com
An online guide to vegetarian restaurants around the world.

VegEats!

www.vegeats.com/restaurants/
World vegetarian and vegan restaurants directory.

Kosher-Dine

www.kosherdine.com
Kosher restaurants worldwide.

The Original Tipping Page

www.tipping.orgs
Tips on tipping around the world.

AFRICA

Food, Drink and the Culinary Arts of Egypt

www.touregypt.net/food.htm
A background to Egyptian food and dining habits. Follow the link to 'Egypt Month' magazine, which reviews local restaurants.

Food & Drink – Ghana

http://goafrica.about.com/travel/goafrica/
msubfood-ghana.htm
Links to information about Ghanaian food and restaurants.

Bwana Zulia's Guide to Restaurants in Kenya

www.bwanazulia.com/restaurants.html
Brief, forthright round-up of where to eat in Nairobi (despite the title, this site doesn't cover restaurants in the rest of the country)

The Tamarind Group – Kenya

www.tamarind.co.ke
The Tamarind Group runs the two restaurants that most visitors to Kenya will or should experience – the wonderful Tamarind Dhow on the coast, and the Carnivore in Nairobi.

Morocco – Food & Drink

http://goafrica.about.com/travel/goafrica/library/planner/
mor/bl-mor-food.htm
Good links to information about food, drink and culinary etiquette in Morocco, with articles on the importance of the tea ceremony and a traditional feast.

M-Web: Eat Out in South Africa

www.mweb.co.za/food/eatout/search.asp
Extensive, searchable database of South African restaurants, with links to their home pages where possible.

South African Wine Directory

www.wine.co.za
Discover the now-famous wines, wine routes and wineries of the Western Cape.

Franshhoek

www.exinet.co.za/wine2/frshoek/index.htm
A guide to wine farms and restaurants in the Valley of the Huguenots, a notable wine region in South Africa.

Food in Tanzania

www.jtarquin.com/sabbatical/travelGuide/tanzania/food.html
One man's view of eating out in Tanzania – a useful article on what to expect in the way of culinary delights.

Tunisian Cuisine

www.tourismtunisia.com/eatingout/cuisine.html
A look at Tunisian cooking, plus restaurants around the country.

ASIA

Dining Asia

www.diningasia.com
A guide to discos, dancefloors and diners throughout Asia-Pacific.

ABC of Arabic Cuisine

www.arab.net/cuisine/
A look at popular Arabic dishes, with a very useful glossary.

Indian Food Guide

www.tadka.com
More recipes than restaurants, but an extremely useful site for learning about the culinary traditions and dishes of different Indian regions.

Makan Time

www.sintercom.org/makan/index.htm
There are approximately 4,000 restaurants in Singapore – and over 17,000 food stalls. This lively unofficial guide doesn't review all the options but does give a great overview of Singaporean food, culture and etiquette, and has halls of fame and shame for the best and worst restaurants.

PHOOD.com

www.phood.com
A guide to restaurants in and around Manila in the Philippines.

Taipei Restaurant Review

www.geocities.com/thetropics/cabana/7031/dining/dine_
index.html
*A round-up of restaurants in Taipei, serving every kind of cuisine
from German to Korean.*

The Ultimate Bangkok Dining Guide

www.v-media.co.th/dining/
*Danish, Egyptian, Irish – every kind of restaurant in Bangkok is
listed here. Not bang up to date though.*

Tokyo Food Page

www.bento.com/tf-rest.html
*Eating and drinking in Tokyo, information on the different styles
of cooking in Japan, a list of recipes and some insightful articles,
including a look at a traditional Japanese kitchen.*

AUSTRALIA

Best Restaurants of Australia

www.bestrestaurants.com.au
*Produced by Australian publishers deGroots, this is the most com-
prehensive guide to eating out in Oz. Simply click on a region on
the map and pick a restaurant by cuisine, price range or location.*

EUROPE

Restaurants OMH

www.restaurantsomh.com
*Reviews of restaurants in London, Paris, Venice, Rome and
Dublin, written for love not money by gastronomic scribes.*

Restaurant guide to Belgium

www.resto.be
*Comprehensive site. A search for African restaurants with outdoor
terraces found six entries, with comments from diners and, in some
cases, links to the restaurants' websites. Online reservations too.*

Restaurant Services – Budapest Week Online

www.budapestweek.com/restaurants.html
Read reviews of restaurants in Budapest – reservations can be made online.

Czech Restaurant and Bar Guide

www.czrb.cz
A searchable directory of where to eat and drink in this upcoming destination.

Prague – Restaurants

www.travelfirst.com/pays/czeres_e.html
Short introduction to Czech cuisine and reviews of gourmet restaurants in Prague.

Italian Cities – Time Out

www.timeout.com/rome/eat
www.timeout.com/florence/eat
www.timeout.com/venice/eat
The best places to eat in the best Italian cities from one of the best names in the business.

The Geneva Restaurant Guide

http://anthropologie.unige.ch/resto.guide/
Unofficial, informative guide to eating out in Geneva.

Salzburg Information Restaurants

http://fmdb.salzburginfo.at/restau/frame_inner_d.htm
Searchable directory of restaurants in Salzburg.

France: Reserve the Best

www.reservethebest.com
Comprehensive listing of restaurants in Paris and the Riviera.

Real France: Art de la Table

www.realfrance.com/rt/artm.htm
French restaurants and food tours, and a look at the famous culinary traditions of the country.

Paris – Time Out

www.timeout.com/paris/eat
Comprehensive guide to the culinary delights of the French capital.

Eat Germany

www.eat-germany.net
Over 23,000 gastronomic addresses throughout Germany, Austria and Switzerland.

Harden's Guides

www.hardens.com
You have to register as a member for access to in-depth details on dining in the UK.

London restaurant directory

www.where-to-eat.co.uk/home.htm
Links to selected restaurants in London.

UK Restaurant Guide

www.taste.co.uk/eatingout/
Details for over 25,000 restaurants, cafés and pubs all over the UK.

Eating & Drinking in Spain & Portugal

http://gospain.about.com/travel/gospain/cs/eatingout/
index.htm
A good assortment of links to related articles and information.

NORTH AMERICA

Canada's Restaurant Guide

www.restaurant.ca
Detailed guide to dining in Canada – search for a restaurant by area or price range.

DineBC.com

www.dinebc.com
Database of nearly every restaurant in British Columbia, Canada.

Diners in the US

www.dinercity.com
Click on a state for details of local diners – or take a look at reviews and a picture gallery of these quintessentially American hang-outs.

Dine Site

www.dinesite.com
Choose a city from the drop down menu, or browse by state for a fairly comprehensive collection of restaurants in the United States.

Dining Guide to LA

www.mdining.com
Extensive listing for restaurants in Tinseltown.

Epinions

www.epinions.com/rest
Reviews of US restaurants by consumers.

Restaurant.com

www.restaurant.com/index.asp
Not just a pretty face – this is a useful, extensive, searchable directory of restaurants in the US.

Restauranteur

www.restauranteur.com
Search for restaurants in California and Colorado on this site produced by the American Culinary Foundation.

Restaurants America

www.restaurantsamerica.com
If you can get past the terrible music, click on a state for reviews and links to restaurants. Coverage can be patchy – there are currently no links for Wyoming for instance, but there is a complete guide to Kentucky.

Shamash's Kosher Restaurant Database

www.shamash.org/kosher/
Kosher dining in the USA.

ENTERTAINMENT AND CULTURE

What's On When

www.whatsonwhen.com
Truly brilliant site with details of events and festivals all over the world. Searchable by theme or country, it covers everything happening everywhere – including Antarctica.

Culture Kiosque

www.culturekiosque.com
European-based guide to arts and entertainment worldwide.

National Holidays

www.national-holidays.com
To make sure that your destination is open for business or partying, check here for bank holidays and events around the world.

Festivals.com

www.festivals.com
Fast becoming an ultimate online destination for festival fans and cultural tourists worldwide, this site covers local fiestas around world, from running with the bulls in Pamplona and the carnival in Rio to more obscure fun.

The Worldwide Holiday & Festival Site

www.holidayfestival.com
Look under countries for forthcoming bank holidays and festivals, or just have a browse – this site is full of interesting links and cultural information.

Worldwide Events

www.wwevents.com
Comprehensive events guide for Europe, the USA and Australasia.

Festpass

www.festpass.com
Europe from festival to festival – over a thousand of them.

Italiafestival

www.italiafestival.it
handy guide to the arts, music, theatre, dance and assorted events in this culture-rich country.

Froots Festivals

www.froots.demon.co.uk/festivals/
Details for hundreds of folk, roots and world music festivals held in Britain and Europe.

Finland Festivals

www.festivals.fi/english/index.html
58 festivals and 20,000 performers spanning across all art forms.

Global Tickets

www.globaltickets.com
Tickets for theatre and entertainment in Europe, Israel and the USA.

Ticketmaster

www.ticketmaster.co.uk
Book online for arts, entertainment and sporting events in the UK, or try www.ticketmaster.com for American events.

World Entertainment Ticketing Centre

www.ticketclic.com
Buy the best available tickets for events in Canada, the USA, France, Italy and Belgium.

Theatre Direct International

www.theatredirect.com
Theatre Direct will book group or individual tickets for shows in London and New York, and can also make restaurant reservations.

Events Worldwide

www.eventsworldwide.com
For details of venues, dates and buying tickets for arts, sport and entertainment events around the world.

Ministry of Sound

www.ministryofsound.com
Click here to link up with their 'Clubbers Guide to…Travel', which covers international destinations.

World Heritage List

www.unesco.org/whc/heritage.htm
A potted guide to UNESCO World Heritage Sites.

Art Republic

www.artrepublic.com
Take a look at the 'What's On Worldwide' section for major art exhibitions and museums around the world.

Worldwide Arts Resources

http://wwar.com/index4.html
Primarily for commercial artists, but a great gateway to museums, galleries and theatre around the world.

African Cultures

http://africancultures.about.com/mbody.htm
Assorted links and articles to a wealth of information on African customs, languages, drama, religion and music.

Indian Culture

http://indianculture.about.com/mbody.htm
An excellent, exhaustive collection of links and features on all things Indian from films and festivals to religion and mythology.

Divine Digest

www.divinedigest.com
A reference guide to the major world religions.

Chapter 5: **The cyberworld** ❧

by Chris Martin

A GLOSSARY OF WEBSPEAK

I̲T̲ ̲I̲S̲ ̲W̲O̲R̲T̲H̲ ̲N̲O̲T̲I̲N̲G̲ that the word 'internet' is a catch-all term for the various parts that make up the online world.

Some technical terms used below

Email (Electronic mail) is a system for sending text messages between individuals who are assigned their own address.

FTP (File Transfer Protocol) is a way of sending files quickly between servers.

Usenet is a giant online bulletin board containing thousands of themed newsgroups. Each newsgroup contains a collection of postings on that topic.

World Wide Web is the network of magazine-style websites consisting of graphical pages connected by hyperlinks. This is what most of us think of when we talk about 'the internet'.

The glossary

Applet A small program, built in Java script, which is downloaded to your PC where it runs independently in a web page.

Attachment A separate file, such as a Word document or an image, which rides on the back of an email message.

Bandwidth The term describing how much information can be carried by a network or the connection between networks.

Banner A graphical advertisement that appears on a web page. Often hyperlinked to the website or service it advertises.

Bookmark A web address saved by your browser which allows you to link quickly to a favourite website. Also known as a 'favourite'.

Boolean system A system of logical expressions which allows advanced users to create refined searches.

Broken link A hyperlink that does not work due to incorrectly written code or an expired destination.

Browser A program that acts as a window to the internet. It presents graphically the code downloaded from a website.

Cache A directory on your hard drive in which your browser stores information, text and graphics that have been downloaded from websites.

Client Any piece of software that downloads information from the internet, whether from the web, your email server or a newsgroup.

Cookie A small file sent by a server that stores itself on your hard drive. A cookie will pass the server information about you when you return.

Cybercafé A café offering internet access on a pay-by-the-hour basis, as well as refreshments.

Cyberspace A slang term referring to world of digital information that is the internet.

Dial-up Connecting to the internet via a telephone line and a modem, usually to an ISP.

Digital certificate A form of accredited financial ID card for e-commerce websites. Your browser can check this certificate to verify the identity of a secure website.

Domain name The distinctive name given to a server which also serves as its web address.

Downloading The action of copying files from a server to your hard disc. The reverse process (sending files from your hard disc to another computer) is called 'uploading'.

DNS (Domain Name System) The operation which converts the numerical system of identification used between computers to a user-friendly domain name.

E-commerce (Electronic Commerce) The buying and selling of goods or services on the internet.

Encryption A process whereby information is scrambled to be transferred securely (such a credit card details).

FAQs (Frequently Asked Questions) Often the help section of a website, employing a question-and-answer format to explain as clearly as possible the functions of the site.

Flaming Rebuking a fellow net user who has annoyed you with a disagreeable opinion or a breach of netiquette. This cathartic activity takes the form of a sternly worded email.

FTP (File Transfer Protocol) The standard computer protocol for transferring raw files across the internet.

Frames Separate independent windows displayed by a website within a single browser window.

GIF (Graphics Interchange Format) A type of image file commonly displayed on websites.

Hits A measure of the individual packages of information downloaded to make up a web page; often used as a measure of user traffic though a website.

Home page The first or front page of a website.

HTML (Hypertext Markup Language) The computer code used to build websites; it tells your browser what to display.

HTTP (Hypertext Transfer Protocol) The system of rules used by computers to transfer information around the internet.

HTTPS (Hypertext Transfer Protocol Secure) The protocol used for handling secure transactions online.

Hyperlink (Link) A highlighted line of text or a graphic in a web page which, when clicked, sends the user to a separate but related page or part of the page.

Image map A large image, areas of which can be clicked as hyperlinks to go to other relevant pages.

IRC (Internet Relay Chat) A small, fast-paced program which allows groups of users to exchange text messages in real time.

ISP (Internet Service Provider) A company that connects individual computers to the internet.

Java A programming language used to create tiny programs called applets that run independently within web pages.

JPEG (Joint Photographic Experts Group) A type of image file commonly displayed on websites.

Keywords A set of words used to describe the contents of a web page. Held in hidden metatags, they help search engines to locate the site.

Leased line A high bandwidth connection between a user and their ISP, which is permanently connected.

Mailbox The directory on your hard drive into which your email messages are downloaded.

Mail server The computer at your ISP where your email is sent and stored until you download it.

Metatags Hidden information about a website contained within its HTML code.

Modem (Modulator Demodulator) A piece of hardware used to convert digital information into sound, thus connecting to the internet via a telephone line.

MPEG (Motion Picture Experts Group) A format for the delivery of high quality video material via the internet.

Netiquette An informal set of behavioural rules for web users.

Network A group of connected computers which communicate with each other.

Newbie Someone new to the internet.

Newsgroup A collection of messages posted to a news server on a topic. Thousands of these discussions make up Usenet.

Newsreader A piece of software used to search and access Usenet newsgroups.

Password A distinctive combination of letters and numbers often used in combination with a user name or email address to identify individual users to a server.

Plug-in An additional piece of software that adds enhanced functionality to your browser.

POP3 (Post Office Protocol) The email protocol that allows you to pick up email.

Portal A website that acts as a gateway to the internet.

Protocol The set of rules which computers must follow to perform specific actions.

Query A request for information from a database.

RAM (Random Access Memory) Your computer's short term memory.

Router A piece of hardware making the connection between servers.

Search engine A database website, which allows you to search for other websites.

Server A computer that stores information and makes it available to the internet.

Spam Junk mail received in electronic form.

Spider A program that travels through the internet seeking out and indexing new websites.

SSL (Secure Sockets Layer) Security technology which is based on the machine code buried deep within a server. The basis of secure e-commerce transactions.

Thread A particular theme of discussion in a newsgroup.

Thumbnail A compact version of a larger graphic, displayed thus to decrease download times.

TLA (Three Letter acronym) Netspeak for abbreviations of internet words, such as 'ISP', 'SSL' – or 'TLA' itself.

Uploading See 'Downloading'.

URL (Uniform Resource Locator) The standard address format for a website.

Webcam A camera which takes pictures at set intervals and publishes them live on the internet.

Web page An HTML document that can include text, images, sounds and movies, plus links to other web pages and files.

Website A collection of web pages on the same server, usually connected by links.

Web space A portion of a server's memory devoted to storing websites.

Wizard An application, often found within another piece of software, which offers interactive help.

WWW (World Wide Web) The graphical, multimedia portion of the internet populated by web pages. ❧

SETTING UP YOUR SYSTEM

To access the internet you will require a computer, a modem, a telephone line, some software and an account with an ISP.

Choosing a computer

Technically it is possible to connect almost anything to the internet, from a five-year-old PC to a brand new WAP phone. In practice, everything will go smoother and faster if you invest in decent equipment. Hardware and software develop so fast that a computer that is adequate now will be frustrating in 12 months time. Always invest in the best equipment you can afford.

When purchasing a computer you should pay attention to the following specifications: its operating system, the processor that runs the operating system, and the quantity of memory.

PC or Mac?

Whether you choose to buy a PC or a Macintosh is largely a matter of personal preference. Those interested in graphics and multimedia prefer working with a Macintosh. But PC is by far the most popular (and cheapest) choice worldwide. You may come across certain problems networking a PC with a Macintosh or vice versa, and there are certain games and programs which are available only to one platform or the other. So it may prove wise to use a similar platform to the majority of your fellow-users and work colleagues. The internet itself is a level playing field: both Mac and PC will navigate it with equal ease.

Should you choose to buy a PC, make sure that it runs Windows 95 or higher, has Pentium II chip or higher and at least 64 megabytes of RAM (memory). Should you choose to buy a Macintosh, make sure that it is a PowerPC, a G3 or above and that it runs System 8 or higher. Again, at least 64 megabytes of RAM is recommended.

Laptop or not?

In terms of processing power and screen size, there is really no difference between desktop and laptop computers any more. For internet users on the move, a laptop has obvious advantages. When purchasing a laptop, check that the keyboard set-up is comfortable for you to use and not too cramped. The battery should allow a decent period of usage before it needs to be recharged (at least three hours).

Remember, too, that you will be the one who has to carry it on the road, so something light and not too bulky is a bonus.

Choosing a modem

To connect to the internet you will need a modem (modulator demodulator). This clever device converts the digital information from your computer into analogue sounds so that data can be transmitted and received through any telephone line.

You may have the choice of a built-in modem or a small, stand-alone box that connects to your computer. While an external modem will be easier to upgrade, an internal modem is more portable and convenient for the traveller.

Speed, as always, is the key. Modem speed is judged by the amount of Kilobits they can deliver per second (KBPS); a decent speed at time of writing is about 56/6.

Choosing an ISP

Most users do not connect directly into the internet. Instead they dial into the computers of an ISP (Internet Service Provider). An ISP is the middleman who connects you into the backbone of the internet proper via a local telephone number.

As well as acting as a gateway and intermediary to the internet, your ISP will also provide you with technical support, any necessary software you'll need to dial into their service, and access to Usenet (newsgroups). It should also handle your email. They may even throw in some free web space for you to build your own website.

There are essentially two kinds of ISP: those who offer a free service, and those who levy a small monthly charge (between £5-£10) to use their service. Why would you pay for a service that you could get free elsewhere? The answer is service.

Free ISPs are not actually free. Essentially you may 'pay' for your access by being bombarded with advertisements or being referred to e-commerce sites of their choice. Furthermore you may charged at premium rate for phone calls made to their technical support line, or for additional services such as web space or multiple email accounts. Some free ISPs are so popular that they can get congested at peak times, which makes logging on difficult and frustrating.

An ISP that you pay for will provide all the above as part of the package, plus guarantees about net access and service levels.

Shop around to find a service that best fits your internet usage. Even if you can't decide, there's nothing to stop you installing more than one ISP or cancelling your account at any time. ❧

TAKING IT ON YOUR TRAVELS

THE INTERNET IS A TRULY GLOBAL SYSTEM, so the software that you will encounter in Birmingham will be much the same as what you might find in Bombay. As a result, the majority of problems you might find in getting online abroad will tend to be rooted in the physical infrastructure of the host country itself –typically its electricity supply and telephone service.

Check your kit

Before you set off, do a little research on your destination. Will you need an adapter to plug your computer into an electrical plug or a phone line? Can your computer's transformer handle the local electrical currently safely? When travelling off the normal tourist route is there a decent telephone network? If not, and the local lines run through a satellite dish, how reliable is their uplink?

Remember that the number which your computer uses in the UK to connect to the internet will be local to your ISP, and therefore expensive to access while abroad. For convenience and cost savings, larger ISPs, like AOL (www.aol.com) or Compuserve (www.compuserve.com), offer alternative international numbers, so that you can dial a local number from wherever you are. Check with your ISP to see if they offer such a service.

Cybercafés

Cybercafés have revolutionised how we communicate when we travel. A cybercafé is a cafe or bar that rents out computers by the hour and also serves refreshments. Popular with tourists and locals alike, cybercafés have become ubiquitous in most cities. Indeed, with a web-based email account and a carefully planned route, you may not need to haul a potentially stealable laptop around with you at all.

Cybercafés are springing up all the time. You can find decent searchable listings of them online at The Internet Café Guide (www.netcafe.com). Such sites are searchable by country and city, and indicate the rates and facilities that are offered by individual cafés.

You can expect to find current web browsers and email clients installed on cybercafé computers. There should also be some wordprocessing software available, though an expensive graphics set-up – sufficient to maintain a website, for example – may be less likely.

In general, if you intend to reconfigure a cybercafé's machines or install a program, don't forget to ask the management.

A good tip is to carry a couple of IBM-formatted floppy discs with you. You can use them to carry your internet bookmarks or details of your home POP3 server (for collecting email). They can also be used to store information picked up on the way, or for keeping a diary.

Web-based email

Web-based email is an email system which is run through a web page. It is efficient, easy to use and absolutely free. A web-based email account has all the features of a regular email client, allowing the user to send, receive and forward email and attachments. But because it is accessible through the open internet rather than through your personal connection to your ISP's email server, you can connect to it from any computer that has a browser installed.

There are hundreds of web-based email services to choose from, hosted by everyone from BT to Elvis Presley's Graceland estate. However, the first – Hotmail (www.hotmail.com) – is still the most popular (within six months of launching it had over half a million subscribers) and it is still the best.

To create an account, you simply call up their website and fill in a few details about yourself. You then choose a username, which will double as your email address. For example, if your username is 'johnsmith', then your email address will be 'johnsmith@hotmail.com'. You also choose a password to protect your mailbox's privacy.

Signing up takes a matter of minutes. You simply return to the same website to pick up or send further email. You can even configure your regular email client at home to automatically forward any incoming mail to your web-based account.

The few problems with web-based email are created by its popularity. The sites are sometimes difficult to log into when busy. You may also have trouble getting your first choice of user name. Be warned, too, that unused accounts are deleted after six months to free up the server space.

These small problems are far outweighed by the convenience of being able to walk into any internet café and pick up your mail. In fact, so popular has web-based email become that cybercafés have become something of a social venue as well as a necessity for travellers of all ages.

WAP, PDAs and other gadgets

PDAs are Personal Digital Assistants, such as Palm Pilots or Psion organisers. WAP stands for Wireless Application Protocol, a software system that allows cellular phones to access the internet on the move. Both bits of kit are excellent for handling email. However, they suffer from small screen-size and slow modem speed through the mobile telephone network, so serious surfing is impractical at present.

Rather than the internet proper, both devices actually connect to WAP- or PDA-enabled portals – a cut down, graphically light version of the original website.

The most efficient way of using a PDA is by connecting it to the internet via your computer. This allows a larger, faster download, for example of an entire travel guide, into the machine's memory. This information can then be recalled offline but on the move.

Theoretically you can buy an airline ticket or book a hotel room with one of these gadgets, using your credit card or an account linked to your telephone bill. But for the moment this is more trouble than it is worth. Despite the hype surrounding 'palmtops', they are aimed squarely at the business user and are of limited use to the general traveller. ❧

TROUBLESHOOTING TIPS

THE INTERNET HAS BECOME SO COMMONPLACE in our lives that it is easy to forget that the system is still in its infancy. It is inevitable that there will be some teething problems. Below are a few of the most common.

When troubleshooting, it is always worth remembering that a bit of common sense is often more useful than a degree in computer science.

Trouble with your modem

Even for the most experienced computer-user, the answer to most problems relating to hardware is 'Have you remembered to switch it on?' Silly though it sounds, it is always worth checking that everything is plugged in correctly before you panic. Here are three quick tips for your modem:

1) Have you configured your internet account? If not, look for the internet start-up wizard on your desktop or consult the help files in your browser for details.

2) If you are receiving no answer from your ISP, are you di-alling the correct number and do you have to add any extra digits for your location (for example, an international code)?

3) If your modem connects to your ISP but then displays an 'authorisation error', are you using the correct user name and password? Remember, too, that these are often case-sensitive.

Trouble with your browser

The two most common browsers, Netscape and Internet Explorer, appear to do the same thing but in fact display web pages using slightly different methods. This means that the same page may look different in each browser, and that dynamic features within a page may work within one browser and not the other.

Fonts

If you find the font size on a page too small or too big, this can be adjusted by the browser itself. Look under the 'View' menu in the browser's toolbar to increase or decrease the font size.

Security

Your browser is designed to filter out undesirable material and to spot dangerous-looking code, which may damage your computer or contain a virus. If your browser security is set to its highest setting, you may find that experimental or ambitious sites cannot load. Security levels can be adjusted in the 'Preferences' menu in your browser's toolbar.

Plug-ins

You will come across certain applications embedded in web pages, such as animations or interactive features, that your browser cannot run without extra software. These additional chunks of software are known as 'plug-ins'. When a plug-in is required, your browser will display an icon in the place of the missing software. Click on the icon and your browser will search for the required plug-in, either by connecting to the internet or by requesting you to insert the relevant system disc.

Trouble with websites

The actual code used to build and publish websites has become more complex as the internet has matured. More complex code allows a website's owners to incorporate extra functionality into their pages, which is very useful, but it can also cause problems for the site's users.

Often, when all or part of a site won't load into your browser, it is the software itself that is out of sync with the code. The easiest way to get around this is to ensure that you always use a reasonably up-to-date browser to start with. At the time of writing, this means Internet Explorer 4 or Netscape Communicator 4 or above. Contact your ISP; they will supply you with upgrades when required.

We've already seen that browsers can be configured to make web pages easier to read. They can also be adjusted for security or speed, but this is best left to the experts, as fiddling with these settings may result in your browser having trouble accessing some websites. Default settings are fine for most of us.

Trouble with cookies

Cookies are small text files sent by a website, which contain information about you that the site will need on your return. This might be details of your shopping account or a membership name and password.

If you are having trouble accessing a site that uses cookies, it may be that the site can't find the necessary cookie on your hard drive. Your browser may be set to reject all cookies, or you may have inadvertently deleted the cookie file from your computer while flushing your memory cache.

Unless you have a specific reason for not wanting cookies stored on your computer, make sure that your browser can receive them. They make life a lot easier. If you have lost your cookies, don't panic. You may lose some account information with certain sites, but you can always register again, and you will still be able to log into the member's area if you have kept a record of your details elsewhere. ❧

NETIQUETTE

NETIQUETTE IS A SLANG TERM for the unwritten code of behaviour between net-users, with particular reference to the protocol between people when communicating online. The phrase has its roots in the themed discussion groups of Usenet, called 'newsgroups'. A single newsgroup may run to several hundred postings, with subscribing members receiving dozens of messages every day by email. To keep the standard of conversation high and to avoid ill-informed, abusive or repeated contributions, netiquette sprang up. The house rules for each discussion are usually available in an 'FAQ file' posted in each group.

When researching any trip, personal recommendations are the mortar that holds together the bricks provided by guide books. Travellers are always happy to talk about their adventures and equally keen to warn of their disasters. The internet offers a huge body of such experience to draw on (there are over 25,000 newsgroups alone), which is simply too good to ignore.

Chat rooms

Larger commercial chat rooms, or those hosted by portals, tend to be moderated. This means that a human editor monitors the discussion, to stimulate interesting interaction and to deal with troublemakers. The moderator will warn or even ban certain users from taking part, if they breach the house rules.

Usenet

Usenet is made up of tens of thousands of individual ongoing discussions called 'newsgroups'. Within each newsgroup you will find hundreds of messages posted by users ('postings'), which look not dissimilar to email. These messages will also be collected together in themes of discussion called 'threads'.

Newsgroups are monitored by the users themselves. Make a nuisance of yourself here and you will be ignored, at best, or more likely 'flamed'. Flaming is the practice of sending a stern email rebuke telling the recipient what's what. These are not pleasant to receive.

Apart from that, don't be too worried about breaching netiquette. Largely it is for your benefit. The usual guidelines you should follow are as follows. Be reasonably polite to other users. Stick to the declared topic in a discussion. Do not repeat large chunks of other people's messages in your reply. Do not attempt to advertise or sell products or services by masquerading them as genuine recommendations. Do not deliberately offer misinformation. Anyone following these simple, sensible rules should find themselves benefiting from an excellent global resource.

Netiquette is all about keeping your interaction with other web users safe, informative and fun. Be polite, be friendly and enjoy yourself – and you may find that a visit to a newsgroup is worth a dozen guide books. ❧

VIRTUAL COMMUNITIES

IT IS NOT SURPRISING that in an environment as diverse and far reaching as the internet, people tend to organise themselves into groups that share interests and opinions. Joining a 'virtual community' saves time when researching a subject – and it's a great way to meet like-minded people online.

Mailing lists and web rings

You might like to start by checking whether your favourite site runs a mailing list. By submitting your email address to the site's publishers, you will receive a monthly or weekly email informing you of updates, offers and events on the site.

A website can also be a jumping-off point if it is a member of a 'web ring'. A web ring is a collection of websites selected by an enthusiast. The ring logo is displayed at the foot of the home page, from where you can follow a hyperlink onto the next site on the ring, back to a previous site, or jump to one at random.

Usenet

If you are looking for more human interaction, you should investigate Usenet. Usenet is essentially a huge bulletin board consisting of over 50,000 individual themed discussions called 'newsgroups'. Each newsgroup covers an individual topic; for example 'Russia'. Within that newsgroup, dozens of 'postings' will be displayed. Each posting is a text message that addresses a particular topic; for example 'The weather in Moscow'. Users can read and post messages in reply to these postings in an ongoing discussion called a 'thread'.

Usenet can be accessed either through a dedicated piece of newsreading software or though a newsgroup website. The drawback with these discussions is their speed. You won't get an immediate reply to your posting. In fact many newsgroup users prefer to download an entire day's postings in one go to browse and reply to them at their own pace.

Chat rooms and IRC

Chat rooms offer real-time discussion. Normally hosted by a website, a chat room will let you type messages to other users on a topic related to the website. Of course, a chat room is only fun if you have someone to chat to. Their proliferation online and the inevitable difficulties of global time differences mean that often they are empty. Look out for organised discussions advertised at a specific time: these will sometimes have special guests, and they have the advantage of other users showing up.

The really dynamic chat happens on the IRC (Internet Relay Chat) network. IRC is run using special software and hosted by dedicated servers, which gives it the advantage of being very fast and letting you search for populated discussions. You can even discover whether individual users are online.

The downside is that IRC addicts are real pros. You will need to learn to type fast and get a basic grip on the acronyms and abbreviations, which are commonplace on this system. Though the speed and ferocity of discussion can be daunting, it is well worth making the effort. ❧

INFORMATION AND DISINFORMATION

by Jonathan Lorie

Question: How do you know that what you read on the internet is true?
Answer: You don't.
Question: How do you know who runs the website that you're reading?
Answer: All you know is what they tell you.

THE WORLD WIDE WEB MAY BE HAILED as the greatest tool for information and research that's ever existed, but it has one glaring flaw. The information on it may not be true.

Let me give you an example. A friend emailed me some news that she had downloaded from a medical website. The news came from a doctor in Australia, who reported that a backpacker had been drugged by criminals and had one of his kidneys removed while unconscious. The crooks sold his kidney for a transplant. It was a terrifying story for travellers to Australia.

I was about to publish this news in *Traveller* magazine when an old-fashioned journalistic instinct made me double-check the facts. Never mind that it had come from a friend or even a respectable-sounding doctor. I wanted first-hand confirmation.

I emailed the medical website. They never replied. I called an Australian news agency, who denied the story. I contacted the hospital where the doctor was said to work. They had never heard of her. I concluded that the story was probably more urban myth than hard fact, and I did not publish it.

That was a small example of how easily common gossip can be recycled via the web until it becomes accepted as true. It's Chinese Whispers on a global scale, as fast as a mouse-click and as far-reaching as the world wide web. Look at the host of 'underground' websites, especially from America, publishing celebrity gossip, political paranoia and insider information of various kinds – much of it unproven and unprovable.

How many web users would bother to check such information with first-hand sources? You see it on a website, the website looks well-presented, you think it's true. You take it on trust, just as you do for anything that's printed in a book or newspaper.

And there's the rub. Anything published in a book or newspaper – or on TV or radio – is carefully regulated by a special body of media law. This might seem hard to believe, considering the wilder antics of the tabloid newspapers, but it is so. To put it very simply, the information they publish can be challenged in court if it is not true, and those involved can be punished, usually with a hefty fine. So they do their best to get the facts right.

By contrast, the internet is unregulated. No website has been taken to court on account of its content, so no one knows if the media laws apply. A few ISPs have been scared into withdrawing their service from unsavoury sites, but that is not a legal precedent. Websites have no proven obligation to tell the truth.

So the potential exists for internet information to be inaccurate. But can it also be deliberate disinformation?

Here's an example. You receive an email from a Hollywood film star, begging you to look at their website. Unless you're unusually well-connected, it's unlikely that this will be from who it says it is. But, in a spirit of wild optimism, you access their website for that personal invitation to Beverley Hills – and find goodness knows what tat lurking there, waiting for the unwary.

More worryingly, you receive an email from a friend asking you to sign a petition to the UN about human rights abuses. There's a shocking report and hundreds of signatures from email people. But you've never heard of them, or of the organisation behind the report. So you email the organisation – and find that its email address does not exist. What are you to make of this? Is the 'report' true? Who wants your signature and why?

The short answer is that if it was an anonymous circular dropped on your doormat – which is all it really is – you would not give it the time of day. The beauty – and the danger – of the web is that anyone can buy a website name to front their activities, and the normal guarantees of truthfulness do not apply. ❧

FUTURE DEVELOPMENTS

IN OUR WIRED WORLD, the cities buzz and hum with the growth of digital communications. Almost daily we shoot satellites into the sky in an effort to span every mountain and desert, to achieve global network coverage. On the ground, our engineers work frantically to connect every telephone to a computer, every computer to a television, and every television to goodness knows what, to keep us online anytime and anywhere.

So it is a reassuring thought for the traveller that two-thirds of the world's population still don't live within three miles of a computer; let alone know how to switch one on. How long this situation will continue is unsure, but what is certain is that the choice to visit a place where you are genuinely out of touch is a luxury that is disappearing fast.

Lessons from the past

It is almost impossible to predict where the internet will take us in the next few years. But we can learn a little from its brief past.

Despite the speed at which it has grown, the internet has remained sensitive to the needs of its users. It has had to. Internet users are great gossips and news spreads fast. Services which are useful will thrive and grow. Applications that are difficult to use, unreliable or unnecessary, tend to vanish overnight.

Increasingly, 'small is beautiful' online. The global ambition of the early internet pioneers is being replaced with the realisation that its true strength lies in its localised services and in the ability to unite communities on the ground into a global whole. This is the unique opportunity that the internet offers us: for someone on one side of the planet to gain instant, intimate knowledge and connection with people and places on the other.

Finally, the continuing application of internet technology to multiple hardware platforms, from street kiosks to hand-held text-messaging units, demonstrates that we are still searching for the ideal method to access the internet. We need something which is powerful yet portable, flexible and yet simple to use, cheap to buy yet looking like a million dollars. And the last thing travellers need is to exceed their luggage allowance just to haul a computer around with them. We're still looking for the ideal kit.

More of the same

For the computer user on the move, the internet already serves as bank, guide, travel agent, companion and fixer, as well as a means to stay in touch. We can only assume that this relationship between man and machine will grow from a privilege of the enlightened few to the norm for everyone everywhere.

The fact still remains, however, that the point and pleasure of travel is to experience the world first-hand and not through a screen. While the internet will continue to be a fantastic tool for preparation and research, no webcam or website will ever overtake the sheer joy of 'doing it' – of being there yourself. ❧

FREE TRIAL TRAVEL CLUB MEMBERSHIP

 WEXAS is the travel club for independent travellers. Our 35,000 members enjoy the unbeatable combination of low prices, travel ideas and information, and outstanding service. As a reader of the *Traveller's Internet Guide* you can take out free trial membership and you'll get a 50% discount on your first year subscription. Take a look at all the benefits you'll receive and see how you'll save your subscription many times over.

- ■ Discount rates on airfares, hotels and car hire worldwide
- ■ Annual travel insurance from as little as £59 per year (2001 rates)
- ■ FREE subscription to *Traveller* – the highly acclaimed travel magazine
- ■ Expert services from experienced travel consultants and access to our members-only phone numbers
- ■ Privileged access to VIP airport lounges
- ■ Currency & travellers cheques available by post, commission-free
- ■ Special rates for airport parking
- ■ Discounts at British Airways Travel Clinics
- ■ £50,000 free Flight Accident Insurance with every flight booking
- ■ Bagtag lost luggage retrieval service
- ■ Free international assistance 24 hours a day
- ■ Discounts on local tours and sightseeing worldwide
- ■ Additional benefits for business travellers
- ■ Access to WEXASonline (members-only website)
- ■ Customised round-the-world itineraries
- ■ Quarterly Update newsletter on special offers and discounts

 Complete this form and post today for full details of WEXAS membership and the free trial offer.

WEXAS International, FREEPOST, London SW3 1BR.

Name (Mr/Mrs/Miss/Ms) ....

Address ....

....

Postcode ....

Telephone ....

Email ....

INDEX